An infantry officer, **Colonel S.C. Tyagi (Retd)** was commissioned in the Rajput Regiment of the Indian Army and has held various instructional and staff appointments at the National Defence Academy, the Army War College, and as the Colonel G.S. of a Mountain Division, among others. He took part in the operations of the IPKF in Sri Lanka and voluntarily served in the Kargil war zone during Operation Vijay. He was the Founder Commandant of the Corps Battle School in the Kashmir Valley. He has been a Research Fellow at USI, where he authored his first book, *The Fourth Estate: A Force Multiplier for the Indian Army*.

After retirement from his career of active military service spanning thirty-two years, Col Tyagi has served in the Ministry of Electronics and IT and as a Cyber Consultant with the Government of India at the apex level. He recently designed an online cyber security fundamental hygiene course for the Common Service Centres. He is the founder and President of the National Association for the Blind, Meerut and the co-founder of Setu, in Delhi, both not-for-profit organizations working in the field of disabilities.

# The Kargil Victory
## Battles from Peak to Peak

Colonel S.C. Tyagi (Retd)

SPEAKING TIGER PUBLISHING PVT. LTD
4381/4, Ansari Road, Daryaganj
New Delhi 110002

First published in India by Speaking Tiger in paperback 2019
Copyright © United Service Institution of India 2019

Photographs and maps courtesy the author

ISBN: 978-93-89231-08-3
eISBN: 978-93-88874-96-0

10 9 8 7 6 5 4 3 2 1

All rights reserved.

No part of this publication may be reproduced,
transmitted, or stored in a retrieval system, in any form or
by any means, electronic, mechanical, photocopying,
recording or otherwise, without the prior
permission of the publisher.

This book is sold subject to the condition that it shall not,
by way of trade or otherwise, be lent, resold, hired out,
or otherwise circulated, without the publisher's
prior consent, in any form of binding or cover
other than that in which it is published.

This book is dedicated to
all the soldiers who took part in the Kargil war
in keeping with the promises made to them
before, during and after the operations.

# Contents

| | |
|---|---|
| *Timeline* | x |
| *List of Maps* | xvii |
| *Preface* | xix |

## BOOK I
## MY KARGIL DIARY

| | |
|---|---|
| Kargil, 1976 | 3 |
| Kargil, 1999 | 5 |
|     In the Battle Zone | 7 |
|     Over to Batalik | 12 |
|     Mashkoh Encounter | 17 |

## BOOK II
## THE WAR AS IT HAPPENED

### Part I
#### Summer Quest 1999

| | |
|---|---|
| Detection of Intrusion and Initial Response | 21 |
|     Detection of Intrusion in Batalik | 22 |
| In Neighbouring Chorbat La | 27 |
|     Snow Tigers, Led by the Lion of Ladakh | 27 |
| Further North-East in Turtok | 32 |

| | |
|---|---|
| Haneef's Call | 33 |
| Intrusion in Kaksar: In the Shadow of Kargil | 35 |
| South West of Kargil: Dras—Mashkoh | 37 |

## Part II
### Initial Battles

| | |
|---|---|
| Igloos Save the Day | 43 |
| Hotel on the Top: Point 5140 | 46 |
| The Crawlers of Tiger Hill | 50 |
| Warriors of the Mist | 55 |

## Part III
### Victories Begin: Dras Battles

| | |
|---|---|
| Turning the Tide in Dras | 63 |
|     An Indian Tsunami at Tololing | 63 |
| Cavemen at Point 5140 | 73 |
| Huffs and Humps | 75 |
| Rocky Knob | 77 |
|     Thumbs Up to Point 5140 | 79 |
| Call Sign of Colas | 81 |
| Magic at Black Tooth | 84 |
| Proud of Three Pimples | 86 |
| Complex Captured (Point 4700) | 94 |
| The Taming of Tiger Hill | 96 |
| Fall of Grand Mashkoh Hub | 109 |
|     Point 4875 | 109 |

| | |
|---|---|
| Pimple II, Twin Bumps and Ledge in Mashkoh | 113 |
| Ledge Invites Wrath | 115 |

## Part IV
### Battles at Batalik-Yaldor—Chorbat La—Turtok—Siachen

| | |
|---|---|
| Operations in Batalik-Yaldor | 119 |
|     Battle of Jubar Complex | 123 |
|     Revety the Spiderman: Capture of Jubar OP | 127 |
|     Hari in a Hurry: Capture of Jubar Top | 128 |
|     Capture of Jubar Main | 129 |
|     Mharo Desh: Tharu | 130 |
| Battles on the Eastern Flank of Yaldor Area | 131 |
|     Battle of Point 5203 | 131 |
|     Jintu in China Nala | 134 |
| Khalubar and Stangba Ridgelines | 138 |
|     Roar of Allah-hu-Akbar | 138 |
| Lightning Bolt in the Sky at Bunker Ridge | 145 |
|     Aayo Gorkhali! | 146 |
| Rising of the Eastern Star | 150 |
|     Capture of Point 4812 | 150 |
| Stangba—Point 5000—Padma Go—Dog Hill | 153 |
| The Glorious Siachen Glacier: Nothing but Excellence | 155 |
| Epilogue | 158 |
| *An Ode to the Indian Soldier* | 162 |
| *Acknowledgements* | 164 |

# Timeline

| Timeline Kargil | Mashkoh | Dras | Kaksar - Kargil | Batalik-Yaldor | Chorbat La | Turtok | Siachen |
|---|---|---|---|---|---|---|---|
| 1-May-99 | | | | | | Unusual movement of Pakistani helicopters spotted | |
| 2-May-99 | | | | | | | |
| 3-May-99 | | | | Shepherd reports unusual movements in Banju | | | |
| 4-May-99 | | | | Patrol sent out | | | |
| 5-May-99 | | | | | | | |
| 6-May-99 | | | | Capt. Vikrant Desai's patrol sent out | | | |
| 7-May-99 | | | | Troops start arriving | | | |
| 8-May-99 | | | | Acivity commences | | | |
| 9-May-99 | | | | Lt. Surve's Patrol sent out | | | |
| 10-May-99 | | | | | | | |
| 11-May-99 | | | | | | | |
| 12-May-99 | | Intruders noticed at Tololing | | Pakistani shelling of HQ. Operations continue. | | | |
| 13-May-99 | | Troops start arriving | | | | | |

| Timeline | Mashkoh | Dras | Kaksar - Kargil | Batalik-Yaldor | Chorbat La | Turtok | Siachen |
|---|---|---|---|---|---|---|---|
| 14-May-99 | | 8 SIKH start operations towards Tiger Hill | 4 JAT patrol under Lt. Saurabh Kalia sent to Bajrang Post; did not return | | | | |
| 15-May-99 | | 1 NAGA start operations towards Point 5100 and Point Point 5140 | Lt. Amit Bharadwaj's patrol sent; they also did not return | | | | |
| 16-May-99 | Intruders noticed | | | | | | |
| 17-May-99 | | Operations of 1 NAGA and 8 SIKH continue | | | | | |
| 18-May-99 | | | | Paratroops occupy part of Shangruti Ridge | | | |
| 19-May-99 | | | | | | | |
| 20-May-99 | | | | | | | |
| 21-May-99 | | | | | | | |
| 22-May-99 | | 18 GRENADIERS launch attack to recapture Toloing | | Troops start arriving and attempts to capture heights continue | | | |
| 23-May-99 | | Operations continue | | | | | |
| 24-May-99 | Troops start arriving | | | | | | |
| 25-May-99 | | | | | Ladakh Scouts start arriving | | |
| 26-May-99 | | | | | | | |
| 27-May-99 | | | | | | | |

| Timeline Kargil | Mashkoh | Dras | Kaksar - Kargil | Batalik-Yaldor | Chorbat La | Turtok | Siachen |
|---|---|---|---|---|---|---|---|
| 28-May-99 | | IAF helicopter shot down | | Attack on Point 4268 by 1 BIHAR | | | |
| 29-May-99 | | 18 GRENADIERS continue their efforts. | | | Rockfall attack occupied by Major Sonam Wangchuk | | |
| 30-May-99 | | | | | | | |
| 31-May-99 | | | | | | | |
| 1-Jun-99 | | 2 RAJ RIF assigned to capture Tololing | | | | | |
| 2-Jun-99 | | | | | Enemy soldiers attempt recapture of Rockfall. | | |
| 3-Jun-99 | | | | | | | |
| 4-Jun-99 | | | | | | | |
| 5-Jun-99 | | | | | | | |
| 6-Jun-99 | | Operations continue | | | | Lt Haneefuddin attempts Point 5590 | |
| 7-Jun-99 | | | | Attack on Point 5203 begins | | | |
| 8-Jun-99 | | | | Part of Point 5203 occupied by Captain Amol Kalia, 5 PARA | | | |
| 9-Jun-99 | | | | | | | |
| 10-Jun-99 | | | | | | | |
| 11-Jun-99 | | | | | | | |

| Timeline Kargil | Mashkoh | Dras | Kaksar - Kargil | Batalik-Yaldor | Chorbat La | Turtok | Siachen |
|---|---|---|---|---|---|---|---|
| 12-Jun-99 | | 2 RAJ RIF launches attack on Tololing | | | | | |
| 13-Jun-99 | | Tololing recaptured by 2 RAJ RIF. | Prime Minister Atal Bihari Vajpayee visits Kargil | | | | |
| 14-Jun-99 | | | | | | | |
| 15-Jun-99 | | 13 JAK RIF launches attack on Point 5140 | | | | | |
| 16-Jun-99 | | | | | | | |
| 17-Jun-99 | | Capture of Thumbs Up leading to Point 5140 | | | | | |
| 18-Jun-99 | | 13 JAK RIF recaptures Point 5140 | | | | | |
| 19-Jun-99 | | | | | | | |
| 20-Jun-99 | | | | | | | |
| 21-Jun-99 | | | | Point 5203 captured by 12 JAK LI | | | |
| 22-Jun-99 | | 1 NAGA recaptures Black Tooth | | | | | |
| 23-Jun-99 | | | | | | | |
| 24-Jun-99 | | | | | | | |
| 25-Jun-99 | | | | | | | Attack on Point 5770 by 27 RAJPUT begins |
| 26-Jun-99 | | | | | | | |
| 27-Jun-99 | | | | | | | Point 5700 captured |

| Timeline Kargil | Mashkoh | Dras | Kaksar - Kargil | Batalik-Yaldor | Chorbat La | Turtok | Siachen |
|---|---|---|---|---|---|---|---|
| 28-Jun-99 | | Battle for Three Pimples starts: 2 RAJ RIF launch attack on Knoll and Lone Hill; 18 GARH RIF attempt to capture Tommy, Saddle and Point 4700 | | | | | |
| 29-Jun-99 | | Both battalions capture their objectives | | Jubar OP captured by 1 BIHAR; 17 GARH RIF attempts capture of Bump III | | | |
| 30-Jun-99 | | | | 22 GREN attempts foothold between Point 5287 and Point 4812 to capture Point 5287; 12 JAK LI launches attack on Point 4812. | | | |
| 1-Jul-99 | | | | | | | |
| 2-Jul-99 | | | | 1/11 GR attacks Bunker Ridge | | | |
| 3-Jul-99 | | Attack on Tiger Hill (18 GREN and 8 SIKH) | | | | | |
| 4-Jul-99 | Attack on Point 4875 by 17 JAT, 13 JAK RIF and 2 NAGA | 18 GREN surprises enemy and captures part of Tiger Hill Top | | Bunker Ridge recaptured by 1/11 GR | | | |
| 5-Jul-99 | Initial objectives recaptured | 18 GREN and 8 SIKH continue to clear enemy off Tiger Hill. | | Point 5287 on Khalubar Stangba Ridgeline captured by 1/11 GR | | | |

| Timeline Kargil | Mashkoh | Dras | Kaksar - Kargil | Batalik-Yaldor | Chorbat La | Turtok | Siachen |
|---|---|---|---|---|---|---|---|
| 6-Jul-99 | Subsequent objectives recaptured | | | Point 4268 in Jubar Complex captured; Point 4812 on Khalubar captured. | | | |
| 7-Jul-99 | | | | Jubar Top captured by 1 BIHAR | | | |
| 8-Jul-99 | Remnants recaptured | | | | | | |
| 9-Jul-99 | | | | Jubar Complex and Tharu completely captured; Ladkh Scouts capture Padma Go. | | | |
| 10-Jul-99 | | | | Ceasefire | | | |
| 11-Jul-99 | | | | | | | |
| 12-Jul-99 | Pakistani troops to begin withdrawal | | | | | | |
| 13-Jul-99 | | | | | | | |
| 14-Jul-99 | | Pakistani troops to begin withdrawal | | | Pakistani troops to begin withdrawal | | |

| Timeline Kargil | Mashkoh | Dras | Kaksar - Kargil | Batalik-Yaldor | Chorbat La | Turtok | Siachen |
|---|---|---|---|---|---|---|---|
| 15-Jul-99 | | | | | | | |
| 16-Jul-99 | | | | | | | |
| 17-Jul-99 | | | | | | | |
| 18-Jul-99 | | | | | | | |
| 19-Jul-99 | | | | | | | |
| 20-Jul-99 | | | | | | | |
| 21-Jul-99 | | | | Pakistani troops did not withdraw as agreed. | | | |
| 22-Jul-99 | | | | | | | |
| 23-Jul-99 | | | | | | | |
| 24-Jul-99 | | | | | | | |
| 25-Jul-99 | | | | | | | |
| 26-Jul-99 | | | | Operation Vijay terminates. | | | |

# List of Maps

| | | |
|---|---|---|
| 1. | Kargil Battlefield | 9 |
| 2. | Batalik Yaldor Chorbat La | 13 |
| 3. | Dras Area | 39 |
| 4. | Initial Isolation of Tiger Hill | 52 |
| 5. | Tololing | 56 |
| 6. | Capture of Tololing | 64 |
| 7. | Dras Area Features | 78 |
| 8. | Capture of Point 5140 | 81 |
| 9. | Capture of Three Pimples/Area Black Rock | 88 |
| 10. | Capture of Point 4700 Complex | 95 |
| 11. | Tiger Hill Features | 97 |
| 12. | Battle of Tiger Hill | 102 |
| 13. | Battle of Mashkoh | 111 |
| 14. | Yaldor Sub-sector | 120 |
| 15. | Batalik-Yaldor | 121 |
| 16. | Capture of Jubar OP | 124 |
| 17. | Capture of Point 5203 | 132 |
| 18. | Battle for Bump III | 135 |
| 19. | Capture of Khalubar Ridge | 145 |

# Preface
## Kashmir to Kargil

'It is a country where the sun shines mildly, being a place created by Kashyap as if for his glory. High school-houses, the saffron, iced-water and grapes, which are rare even in heaven, are common here. Kailasa is the best place in the three worlds, Himalaya the best part of Kailasa, and Kashmir the best place in Himalaya'.

—*Rajatarangini*

*Rajatarangini* (The River of Kings), a historical account written by Kashmiri poet Kalhana, describes the Valley of Kashmir in the Himalayas as a large lake around which great sages lived. As per legend, Kashmir has its origin in the name of one of these revered sages, Kashyap Rishi. Archaeological finds indicate that civilization existed in Kashmir as early as 5000 BCE.[*] A land of unparalleled beauty, Kashmir assumed geostrategic importance several centuries later, due not only to its natural abundance, but also because of its link to the famous Silk Route that connected Central Asia with China, via Tibet. The fame of its rich caravans attracted an army of invaders who came to conquer and plunder. As Kashmir offered access to the rich plains of Punjab and beyond, as well as to the Silk Route, it

---

[*] Bammi, Lt Gen Y.M. (Retd), 1999. *Kargil: The Impregnable Conquered*, Gorkha Publishers, p. 44.

was a prize conquest. The Kushans, Huns, Tartars, Mughals, Sikhs and Dogras controlled or ruled over this paradise from the mediaeval period onwards.

The Partition of India in August 1947 was one of the greatest tragedies that our planet has seen, as millions of people who shared a common heritage left their homes and family histories, to form separate cultural identities. When it came to Kashmir, its ruler, Maharaja Hari Singh, had been slow to make up his mind about whether to join India or Pakistan. Many attempts were made to influence the Maharaja to accede to Pakistan, but in the end he chose to remain independent.

Within a few months, Pakistan had sent its Raiders to conquer Kashmir. They occupied many parts of both Jammu and Kashmir and took over Gilgit and Baltistan. Threatened by their actions and their rapid advance to Srinagar, the capital city, the Maharaja signed the Instrument of Accession with India. The Indian Army landed in Kashmir to fight the Raiders the very next day, 27 October 1947. The Raiders offered resistance, but soon lost heart and began retreating, even though they were backed up by Pakistani troops.

In Ladakh, most of the existing army forces had fallen back to Skardu, a small town which falls en route to Leh. It was held by a small garrison of men under Lieutenant Colonel Sher Jung Thapa. The garrison was heavily outnumbered and the town was besieged from all sides for the next eight months, before finally capitulating on 14$^{th}$ August, 1948. The Pakistani Raiders also occupied the shoulders of Zoji La* and quickly moved to Dras and Kargil to reach the vicinity of Leh. Once Leh was threatened by a well-entrenched enemy, Major General K.T. Thimayya, DSO, the General Officer Commanding, decided to employ light tanks to regain control over the pass and the road link to Leh. In addition, two relief columns were sent to Leh by different routes.

---

* La means a mountain pass.

Meanwhile, the road from Sonmarg to Zoji La was improved to facilitate the movement of tanks.

A relief column under Major Prithi Chand, 2nd Battalion of the Dogra Regiment, negotiated the frozen landscape, and under hostile weather conditions, managed to reach Leh. Another column reached through the Kullu-Manali-Leh track. Working without much assistance, an airstrip at Leh was created with great difficulty. The first aircraft, flown by Air Commodore Meher Singh, landed on this airstrip on 23rd May 1948.

The tank columns to be employed for the first time at high altitude came from the 7 Light Cavalry, under Lt Col Rajinder Singh 'Sparrow'. Once the track was improvised, the tanks moved up despite bad weather, on 1st November 1948. They destroyed enemy bunkers and captured Zoji La.

The battle in the spring of 1948 had progressed to a level where the Indian Army could have recaptured all of Kashmir, but a United Nations (UN) sponsored cease-fire came into effect on the first day of 1949. There were three main clauses of the UN Resolution: first, to accept and implement a cease-fire; second, to withdraw all Pakistani troops and Raiders from the entire State of Jammu and Kashmir; and finally, both countries were to reaffirm that the future of the state should be determined in accordance with the will of the people.

Both India and Pakistan implemented the first part of the UN Resolution, but the second part was not honoured by Pakistan. Thus, India rejected the proposal to hold a plebiscite until the withdrawal of the Pakistani troops and the Raiders was completed.

Pakistan continues to forcibly occupy parts of Kashmir till date, and harbours designs to annex Kashmir. In 1948, the Raiders held on to a few locations which included Point 13,620, dominating Kargil town on the Srinagar-Leh road. This was later recaptured by the Indian troops under Maj B.S. Randhawa of the 4th Battalion of the Rajput Regiment, when Pakistan attempted to grab Kashmir once again in the 1965 war. However, after this war, an agreement was reached under the guidance of the UN Observers to maintain the status quo of the Cease Fire Line (known as the Line of Control or LC/LOC, after the Simla Agreement of 1971) and Point 13,620 was returned to Pakistan. The Indian Army finally recaptured it from Pakistan in 1971. Such reverses, coupled with the surrender of the Pakistani Army to the Indian Army after the 1971 war leading to the liberation of Bangladesh, continue to hurt the Pakistani psyche.

∼

The occupation of the heights in Kargil that took place in 1999 was a part of Pakistan's overall sinister design to foment trouble for India, avenge Pakistani failures in the past, and ultimately annex Kashmir.

It is the twentieth year after the Kargil war and a large number of books and accounts have already been written and published during this period. Almost every detail of the war is known, but an effort has been made to give the reader additional finer details wrapped in prose.

There are many stories of bravery and courage from the war but it is not easy to compile all of them in just one book. After a period of two decades, the present younger generation needs to be reminded of the tales of bravery of the warriors in Kargil to inspire and motivate them. This account of Kargil war is an effort towards that direction.

The battle in Kargil had several fronts along the Line of Control (LoC) on a frontage of 170 kilometres. For ease of understanding, the whole frontage has been divided into five sectors: Dras-Mashkoh, Kaksar-Kargil, Batalik-Yaldor-Chorbat La and Turtok and beyond, due to the different response mechanisms and control structures. The Kargil war unfolded with the detection of enemy presence in Batalik-Yaldor first and several actions there. The subsequent detection of the enemy in Dras, Kaksar and Turtok further confirmed the large-scale designs of the Pakistani intrusion. Initial reactions were handled by the local commanders over the entire frontage, until the size of the intrusion demanded a greater response from India, and a larger body of troops. The focus shifted from Batalik to Dras, where the enemy threatened the National Highway by occupying Tololing, close by, and Tiger Hill, which was far away but nonetheless directly visible from the highway. In this book, the battles in each front have been kept together and narrated in order, with the clock starting in the month of May 1999.

Storytelling and anecdotal formats have deliberately been used to narrate military matters to make the book readable, especially for the younger generation of today. Facts have been woven in a manner to present the complete picture of the entire valour and its glory, and to give a feel of it happening 'live' in front of them. The scanned photos, wartime pictures, were mostly taken by me with a traditional camera loaded with a film roll, and the picture quality may not be comparable with present-day digital photos. The same goes for the maps, which were hand drawn and saved on computer with the then available tools and technology. Luckily, most of these have survived the onslaught of time. Some of the stories here are included because I could gather more detail about them. I have made an effort to keep them simple and easy to read. To this end, I've tried to follow the chronological sequence of events on the battlefield, rather than the sequence of our visits to the soldiers. In keeping with my promise to the soldiers in Kargil, this effort is a tribute to all of them.

'Wars may be fought with weapons, but they are won by men. It is the spirit of the men who follow and of the man who leads that gains the victory.'

—General George S. Patton

# BOOK I

# MY KARGIL DIARY

# Kargil, 1976

*Pristine nature*
　　*Envelops me,*
*The snow and the wind*
　　*Blind me.*
*All I sense is my lonely self,*
　　*As alone as the man behind me.*

The gruelling Commando Course in the 'happening' town of Belgaum had just concluded. Here I was, a starry-eyed Young Officer (YO), staring excitedly at my very first Posting Order. Kargil, here I come!

A two-night halt at the Transit Camp at Srinagar was followed by a hop onto a Military Convoy. The convoy rolled rather slowly, as they always do, and we revelled in the opportunity of traversing our very own Paradise-on-Earth at leisure. The picturesque green landscape of the Kashmir valley soon gave way to snow-capped peaks. We were now at the Zoji La. The road here wound through snow, already lying heavy over the tracks of the previous vehicle to come this way!

By evening, we were at the base at Kargil. A barren landscape and eerie silence interrupted by flurries of snow greeted us. They were to be our companions from now on, particularly when moved even higher up to an altitude of 18,000 feet as the

Company Post* Commander to a handful of soldiers. Down below was a white blanket, as the clouds mostly settled around Kargil base. Above, the sky was crystal clear and one could see millions of stars shining alongside the beaming moon, which looked much bigger and closer than I had ever seen it before. The weather changed frequently from clear to cloudy to threatening thunder, several times in a day. Nature presented itself on a mighty note, supremely indomitable. Cold winds swept through at high speeds all through the day and night, and the smallest slip by any one of us could send one hurtling thousands of feet below. Temperatures dropped to minus 50, even minus 80 degree Celsius. Everything froze, perhaps even our thoughts! All we were aware of was our immediate surroundings and our desperate ploys for sheer survival. Here, there were only a few trees but none of them bore any leaves. One longed to see the green world, and the welcoming warmth of bustling crowds.

Days rolled into weeks, and weeks into months and then an errand to Kargil gave me a chance to come back down to base. The prospect of interacting with new human beings was reason enough for much happiness. Kargil had some eighty to ninety hutments with a tea stall and a few other shops on the roadside—a mega-city to me! Just a handful of cheerful faces mingling together were enough to create the ambience of a market street and convince me that I was still part of a normal, civilized world.

My return from this frozen moonscape after more than a year gave me a new sense of belonging and respect for the might of nature and Mother Earth. Little did I know then that this experience in Kargil would one day come in handy for me while dealing with the oldest scourge of humanity—war!

---

*A piece of ground occupied by the military which shelters their equipment and personnel, and facilitates training and operations.

# Kargil, 1999

Staring into the valley two decades later, memories of that visit flashed past my eyes. I was now the Founder Commandant of a Corps Battle School raised to deal with terrorism in the Kashmir Valley. Little did we know then that while we were involved in our daily routine of the Battle School, disturbing developments were taking place beyond Zoji La. There were reports of small intrusions at several places. The local troops posted in the Kargil area were dealing with them and the situation did not, then, look alarming. But more troops were being rushed in as the intrusions increased and so did the loss of lives. And then, to my horror, the men under training at the Corps Battle School were also sent there!

Strange, Serious, Sinister—the newspapers and visual media began speculating about the happenings in Kargil and tales started spreading across the country.

A soldier wishes for peace, but always considers himself lucky if he gets a chance to be part of a war effort. I had an opportunity earlier as part of the Indian Peace Keeping Force in Sri Lanka, but the operations there were of a different nature. I felt Kargil beckon to me. This was, after all, where my military career had begun. Perhaps, I would get to gather stories of heroism and valour to narrate to my grandchildren. Perhaps I would inspire young people to serve our motherland!

Thus motivated, I found myself at the doorstep of the highest officer I could report to directly—the Chief of Staff in the Corps

Headquarters in Srinagar. While he appreciated the fact that I had volunteered to go to the troubled area, he was hesitant to permit me to do so. I explained my intent of cataloguing stories from the battlefield for the purpose of analysis and application in future war efforts. Besides, I argued, all the battalions which had been sent there so far had been trained at the Corps Battle School, and as their guru, the rapport that I had built with them would enable me to motivate them further. He was convinced and I was allowed to proceed.

A signal was sent to all the formations in the battle zone to expect my team and to extend all facilities that could assist me in my self-assignment. The word had spread within our own station as well. Even before I could order the packing of my bags, one of my dearest colleagues in the Corps Battle School, Major Ram Singh Kadian (Kady to all of us), stood in the doorway to my office. He was joined by Major Subbiah Kailasam, and they requested me to allow them to accompany me to Kargil. Others, too, lined up after them, with scant regard for their own lives. Such is the spirit of a soldier!

Finally, I conceded only to Kady coming with me, with the others joining me later, perhaps. I didn't wish to dampen their enthusiasm, so the reason I cited was that someone had to look after the Battle School (even though there was no one left there to train!)

## In the Battle Zone

Riding atop a military Jonga* and accompanied by a 3-tonne Shaktiman,† we reached Zoji La. It was time to bid farewell to the

---

\* A heavy-duty version of the military Jeep.

† A military truck.

beautiful Kashmir valley. On the other side of Zoji La, the snow-clad mountains and valleys were stern and bare, without greenery. It was the month of June when heatwaves pummel major parts of India, but freezing temperatures greeted us there. The only road was full of military vehicles and a handful of private trucks, all loaded with military equipment. A camp bustling with activity came into our view. We headed for it and met the Commanding Officer (CO). We were welcomed and advised to stay the night as movement was not easy without headlights: in battle zones it is a rule of thumb to turn them off and avoid making an easy target of yourself.

As the sun set, the Pakistani artillery started shelling.[*] The bombs flew past us, bursting with a loud thundering sound as they landed, and sending shockwaves that shook the ground. While we were alarmed, the soldiers present continued their work as though this was nothing out of the ordinary. Gradually, we realized that the shells were all landing somewhere behind us. We were told that it was a routine affair and the Pakistanis had not been able to find the exact coordinates of the camp yet.

Through that cold night across Zoji La, we heard innumerable stories about the experiences of the soldiers, to the accompaniment of many hot beverages. The only problem was that none of the heat got transferred to our shivering bodies. Eventually, fatigue took over and we dozed off.

Pakistani shelling once again greeted us the following morning. We seemed to be getting used to the sound. It remained biting cold until much later when the sun broke through the mountains, kissing the sky. A welcome sight and sensation! Thus warmed, we resumed our journey towards Dras, our first destination. Despite the heavy shelling targeting any open patches, we encountered

---

[*] Ammunition/bombs consisting of a cylindrical metal casing containing an explosive charge and a projectile are known as shells; they are fired from a large gun.

quite a few loaded vehicles, moving in both directions. Artillery bombs exploded all around us throughout the day, but fortunately always at some distance. We reached Dras by lunch time.

We were struck by the equally cheerful lack of concern about the shelling from the officers and men present at Dras Headquarters (HQ). As a matter of fact, the joke doing the rounds was: 'If you hear the artillery bombs whistling above you, don't worry as they're flying overhead. If you don't hear the sound, again, don't worry; once the bomb hits you, you won't be there to worry!' This became our mantra whenever we encountered artillery shelling thereafter.

I was assigned a bunker underground. It was a dug-out in the ground, covered with a tin shed, which had lots of earth thrown on it. The entrance was a narrow passage and one had to almost crouch to get in. I was told to cover the entrance at night to keep out the cold and any shrapnel from bombs that might land nearby. Seeing my face fall, the Dras officer tried to comfort me, saying that it wasn't that bad. I boldly enquired about an empty hut nearby—couldn't I sleep in it? An emphatic 'no' was the answer—the hut was a 'registered target'\* of the enemy!

I shared my previous experiences in Kargil with the men. After I had fallen asleep at night, the heavy snow had enveloped my bunker and also filled up the passage, jamming the door shut, with me inside. All the other bunkers at my post were in the same situation, with no one outside to dig us out! Fortunately, a pair of sentries realized that something was not quite right and managed to dig us out, one by one. I would rather face enemy bombs than such a fury of nature any day. And, after all, the hut was still intact despite the heavy odds against it! Well, I was a guest and my wish had to be honoured, so I slept in that tin hut

---

\* A target is registered when its coordinates are saved and a number/name is assigned to it; this allows gunners to shoot without wasting time the next time it is targeted.

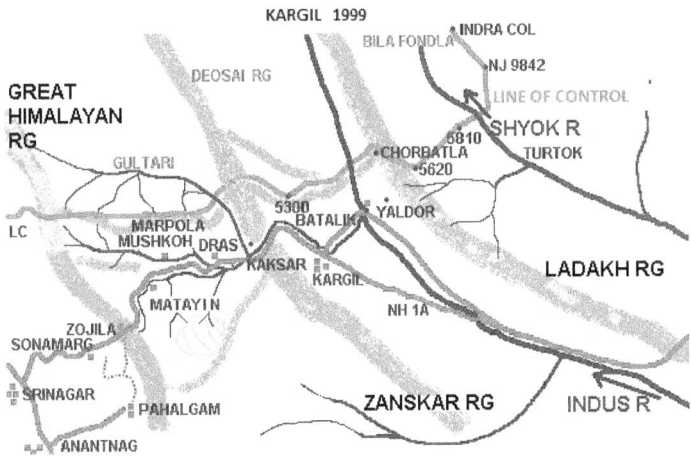

MAP 1: Kargil Battlefield

for the next couple of days, without even bothering about the bombs flying overhead.

Dras was the nerve-centre of all the action. The HQ were tucked in close to one side of the National Highway 1D and dominated by mountains from all sides. The prominent Posts occupied by the Pakistanis included Tololing, Black Rock, Tiger Hill and Point 4875.[*] Tololing was the nearest height; it had recently been cleared of the enemy after a heavy fight. Action at Tiger Hill and Point 4875 was in progress.

I was keen to move up to see the action, but my role did not permit me to interfere in any of the operations. I requested Brigadier Amar Aul, the Dras Brigade Commander, to permit me to go to the Forward Posts, and though he was initially hesitant to allow me to proceed to these areas fraught with danger, he eventually granted permission.

---

[*] A Point is the highest place on a mountaintop. The number following it denotes its height above sea level in metres.

Kady and I took our Jonga up towards a post called Sando. It was a 10-kilometre-long upward journey, right under the nose of the enemy. We were clearly visible from all their posts. En route, we found our own artillery tucked into the mountainside, preparing to fire their guns. They were surprised to see us, but happy to meet new people. Their 'josh' (enthusiasm) was visible and they looked neither tired nor apprehensive. The tips they gave us on to how to escape from enemy artillery shelling while on the move came in very handy throughout our stay in Kargil.

Sando Post was like a table-top at 16,000 feet, with the enemy posts surrounding it. We were greeted by smiling soldiers, seemingly unaffected by their precarious position. The CO was Colonel D.K. Borah, my senior at the National Defence Academy (NDA), who rushed us into a cramped underground bunker where one could barely stand. He was visibly pleased to see us, as no one had been able to visit them for a long time, but surprised that we had not yet been shot down by the hundreds of 'enemy rounds'[*] that had been raining upon them every day during the daylight hours and sometimes at night too. Until then, I had not realized the gravity of the danger we were exposed to.

The CO showed us around and took us to a vantage point from where we were shown Tiger Hill and many other enemy posts, in detail. An elderly moustachioed Junior Commissioned Officer (JCO)[†] was especially introduced to us as he'd been instrumental in saving many lives by giving advance warning about enemy bombs. A towering personality, he had the uncanny knack of being able to sense danger. Intuition, honed and cultivated, perhaps! He stood guard all the while to warn us about any dangers.

---

[*] Artillery bombs.

[†] Naib Subedar, Subedar and Subedar Majors are referred to as JCOs; they act as an interface between the officers and the men, since the British originally needed local officers to communicate with the troops.

We were once again moved to the bunker, where we were surprised to find the Brigade Education Officer and the Medical NCO from the Brigade HQ. He had just arrived, with orders to carry necessary medical equipment for us and back us up when needed. No movement could take place during daylight as Sando Post was constantly in danger of an artillery attack from all directions. Fortunately, it was not within the range of other weapons, such as machine guns. Despite heavy odds, they had not had any fatal casualties, thanks to the strict control exercised by the battalion. The biggest achievement for any battalion commander is not to lose a single man to enemy fire.

Time passed quickly, as we all exchanged quips and stories. As evening approached, the CO suggested that I stay the night. I, however, had to leave for the base at Dras, as I hadn't yet completed my acclimatization period, so it was not possible for me to stay at 16,000 feet any longer. Also, I had other areas to cover. Despite the CO's worry about enemy shelling, we made it back to the base without any bombs landing on us. When we arrived, Brigade Commander Aul hugged us and thanked God for bringing us back without any casualties. He confessed he had not been at rest through the day, fearing he had inadvertently allowed me to go into danger—despite our makeshift but well concealed Officers' Mess* at Dras being right in the shelling zone of enemy artillery!

A little later in the day, we were surprised to see a young woman walk in to the Officers' Mess. She was introduced to us as a TV reporter covering the war—she occasionally took shelter at the base when she got delayed in the evening and wasn't able to return to her hotel in Kargil. A hotel had come up in Kargil, since my last visit!

To complete my acclimatization, I had to stay for a couple of days at Dras. I could travel to visit other posts, as long as I did

---

* A place where everyone collects to relax and have meals together.

not stay overnight on the higher peaks. I used this opportunity to visit the 2nd Battalion of Rajputana Rifles (2 RAJ RIF) and the Grenadier Battalions, not too far away. These battalions had performed miracles and won victories after initially bearing the brunt of the enemy fire.

## Over to Batalik

We stayed at Kargil overnight en route to Batalik a few days later and I couldn't help remarking on the change the hamlet had undergone since I had been there last, twenty years earlier. It was now a small township, with a few shops and the aforementioned hotel, but due to the enemy shelling, the bazaar was mostly closed the day we were there.

The enemy greeted us with artillery bombs as night fell. The shelling did not appear to cause any fear amongst the troops as they knew precisely what areas to avoid, especially during the nights. We were also shown the limits of our safety from enemy shelling. Bombs came from behind Point 13620, which has exchanged hands a couple of times between India and Pakistan. It has been with us since its recapture in 1971. Bombs fell sporadically through the whole night, but they didn't prevent us from falling asleep soon after optimistically wishing each other 'Goodnight, see you in the morning!'

We woke up to a pleasant day, except for the news that some damage had been caused to inhabited huts in the area. Fortunately, there had been no casualties and we headed off to Batalik in good time. I had been there once before, on a long-range patrol in the Chorbat La area. I had a faint memory from then, of being trapped in the snow right up to my neck before the soldiers accompanying me could bail me out. It had taken quite an effort to pull me out. It had felt like a fun-filled adventure then, and was later recounted as a humorous anecdote in the battalion Officers' Mess thereafter, mostly to pull my leg.

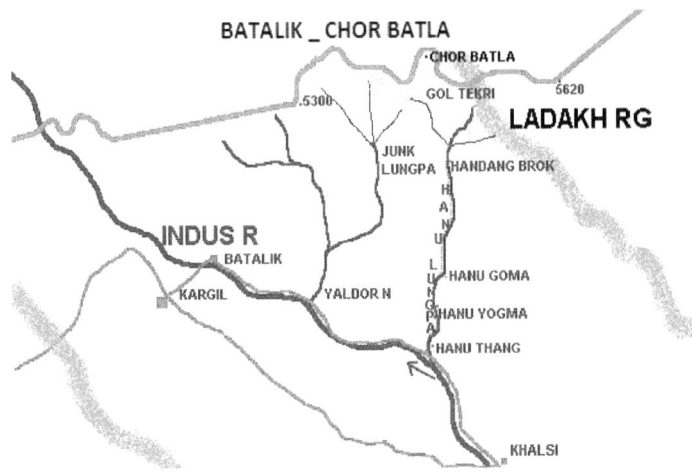

MAP 2: Batalik Yaldor Chorbat La

Upon arrival at Batalik, we were greeted by the 3rd Battalion of the Punjab Regiment (3 PUNJAB) whose Commanding Officer's name, Colonel Vijay Bakshi, resonates with Operation Vijay, the name by which the Kargil operations are known today. The battalion was spread along a narrow road with high peaks to one side and steep falls on the other. Driving along it was extremely dangerous, and any slip meant plunging into the gorges and nalas* below.

After a hot meal, we were taken to a nearby flat area, the size of a football ground, that gave us a panoramic view of the entire sector around. This area had served as the battalion HQ but the sudden breakout of enemy bombardment had completely destroyed it just a few weeks ago. The HQ was now located on the narrow road, which hadn't dampened the energy and spirits of the men it housed at all.

---

*A nala/nullah or simply 'N' on a map is a passage where melted snow or rainwater flows. It's usually dry until water comes down the slopes.

We also found a young doctor attending to the sick and injured. The sight of her braving the high altitudes and miseries of war with a smile must have been very inspiring to the men who fought there. My brief interaction with her made me respect her even more, as I learnt that she had a year-old child who was being looked after by her mother-in-law and her civilian husband, somewhere in Punjab. She was one of the two women officers we met during Operation Vijay.

We had to halt at Batalik when it got dark. Despite our tents, we were told that since the artillery bombardment continues at night, it was not safe to stay outside. They had hurriedly assembled some makeshift bunkers, all tucked into the mountainside along the narrow gorge to prevent enemy bombs falling upon them. Due to the icy winds and even colder temperatures at night, they were made airtight with thick blankets which prevented any light from passing through. I was determined to sleep outside as I didn't like being cooped up without fresh air and starlight, so close to the majestic beauty of nature. Kady, my partner from the Corps Battle School, also tried convincing me that it was too dangerous but I was adamant and had my tent pitched on a slope in the nala. It had to be a little distance away as there was no flat piece of ground available.

I had barely fallen asleep when I heard bombs explode some distance away. A soldier from my battalion came running and shook me out of my slumber. With foggy eyes, I saw water gushing close to my feet. It had rained somewhere in the higher reaches and it was the icy water of a flash flood! Like a cat, I jumped out of my tent. We were able to strike the tent and remove its contents just in time before the water filled up the place. I had to spend the night in the makeshift bunker I'd been offered earlier after all.

The next day, we ventured out to explore the battle area further, travelling along the Indus to catch up with the First Battalion of the Bihar Regiment. They had stabilized the battle in the Jubar complex and were now located close to the river, recuperating from their long battles. They had arrived right in the beginning of the war and had suffered quite a few casualties, including the loss of some very brave officers. We learnt that there was a cluster of villages nearby that took pride in their identity as the only pure Aryans existing in the world. They told us a story of how some Germans had spotted them and wanted to take a bride away, but were politely refused!

The following day we arrived at the HQ of the Batalik Brigade that had been actively engaged in operations ever since the first few days of the war. Brigadier Devinder Singh was deeply involved in the planning and conduct of operations in this region. He was to oversee operations up ahead on a mountain peak, right near the Line of Control (LOC) by helicopter when I arrived. Despite his very busy schedule, he found time to greet us and offered that I could accompany him and see the battle for myself. I, of course, jumped at the opportunity.

When it came, the helicopter brought mailbags that were unloaded while the rotors kept running (a standard practice, since on such heights the engine might fail to re-start due to the low temperatures and lack of oxygen). The blasting bombs could not dampen the soaring spirits of our soldiers as they received and read letters from their loved ones.

As we took off in the helicopter towards the LOC, the sight of the cheerful soldiers receded as we were enveloped by clouds and the windscreen became blinded with snowflakes. The pilots could barely see anything, but negotiated the clouds skilfully. We flew into a gap between two peaks and up ahead on the shoulder of another peak, could see the flat part of the mountain, barely a few hundred square feet, where we were to land. Soldiers were milling around, and presently, they sent up a smoke candle to indicate that it was safe to land. Although the helicopter could be seen by the enemy and effective artillery fire could bring it down, we had to take the chance that they wouldn't be able to get in an accurate hit in the initial volley itself. After that, the helicopter could take off and fly to safety. Of course, there was a chance that we could be stranded on this peak, right in the middle of the fighting, but such a likelihood had to simply be ignored.

The soldiers posted here were Paratroopers from 5 PARA and Ladakh Scouts. They looked even more cheerful than the others we had seen, as the success of their operations so far had been phenomenal. Our helicopter was carrying a bag full of letters for them, as well as some fresh rations to keep them going, and we saw the delight with which they were received. While the Brigadier carried out his inspection, I looked around. Pakistan-Occupied Kashmir (POK) was visible from that point. I couldn't help but be impressed by the tremendous poise and cool demeanour of our soldiers in the face of so much enemy fire. Fortunately, no artillery shells descended on us and we were able to return to the Brigade HQ well before the light faded. From there, the helicopter hurriedly flew back to the base.

A few days later, I was lucky enough to get another helicopter lift to go and brief my seniors about matters in Dras. As the helicopter took off, I looked back and saw smoke and dust rising from the vicinity of the helipad—the enemy had targeted it with his artillery shells! Thankfully, I learnt later, no one was injured at the helipad as it was immediately vacated after the helicopter took off. This was the standard drill, and following it kept many soldiers safe.

I spent the next week there and took a complete round of the Batalik—Chorbat La area. I also took this opportunity to go up to the Mashkoh Valley, where the battle was nearly coming to an end.

## Mashkoh Encounter

While returning from Mashkoh, I was caught in the open, in broad daylight. A military truck was coming from the opposite direction at great speed. It halted for a few seconds and the driver yelled out, signalling to me to not go ahead as there was danger! He then sped past us. I was in no mood to halt, or to go back to Mashkoh which I had left barely an hour ago, so I decided to take a chance and keep moving.

A sudden blast ahead to my right shook the ground and we were enveloped in drifting smoke. Before I could take evasive action, another blast occurred behind us, where we had been a short while ago! The enemy had seen us from one of the heights and was targeting us with his artillery guns, deployed behind the mountains. My military training told me that the enemy was using the 'bracketing' method to correct the fall of his shots upon me. This works by first firing a round, and then calculating the distance and angle to correct the next shot by dropping down a few hundred metres. Once the target is within this bracket, he halves the distance to get the shot spot on you!

If I stopped, I would allow myself to be part of this scheme and definitely fall under his fire. And if the enemy were not found to be bracketing, I might well be shot anyway, since I was clearly in his range already. I had to take a chance! I asked Kady, who was driving me, to speed up ahead for a few seconds, then suddenly slow down, and then repeat the whole process once again, and then, finally, exit the enemy's chakravyu speedily. Those few minutes of evasive action seemed like an eternity before we were able to take our vehicle around a bend where the enemy, we hoped, couldn't observe us! Sure enough, the bombs kept exploding at different levels for the next half an hour or so till it fell dark and we could move on, without our headlights, towards the base at Dras. We had managed without a scratch, except for a flat tyre due to shrapnel from the bombs piercing it! We had changed it quickly on a slope where we were probably not visible to the enemy. Kady laughed all the way, thanking our military training instructors who had taught us well.

Major Kailasam luckily landed at Dras the next day, with a new tyre all the way from the Corps Battle School. He and Kady made another trip safely to the same part of Mashkoh Valley and back, despite our encounter. We stayed on for a couple of days more, but since the Kargil War had nearly ended, I was recalled to resume my duties as the Commandant of the Corps Battle School.

# BOOK II

# THE WAR AS IT HAPPENED

# Part I

# Summer Quest 1999

# Detection of Intrusion and Initial Response

Kargil used to be an unknown hamlet somewhere deep in the Ladakh region of the Himalayas, adjacent to the beautiful Kashmir valley. A few huts dotted the landscape. In the local dialect, the word Kargil means a central place in between many castles. The area connected many kingdoms of the past and therefore served as a key centre between Srinagar, Leh and Skardu, a place in present-day POK. The Zanskar and Suru valleys and Dras are some of the important population centres around it. Kargil fell midway on the journey between Srinagar and Leh on a track via Zoji La. In the past, another foot track through the lofty mountains and passes served the people going between Skardu and Kargil. Batalik lies towards the northeast of Kargil along the Indus River, which ultimately enters Pakistan.

The month of May in Batalik is full of flowers, fruits and gaiety for the handful of Aryan villages along the river. The shepherds have only two months to take their yaks and other animals out to graze in the nearby meadows along the base of the ridgelines before the snow comes back. The ridges are typically sharp here, like shark's teeth, and are joined to form jagged crest lines. The ridgelines do not have paths due to the heavy snow, which can be thirty to forty feet deep during the winters.

## Detection of Intrusion in Batalik

Tashi Namgyal, a shepherd, had gone to search for his missing yak when he found some people in black uniforms moving stones to build a bunker on a high mountainside near Banju. He reported this activity to the local Battalion Commander in the first week of May 1999. Although the information seemed quite innocuous, the commander in Batalik decided to send a patrol* immediately to confirm it. As Banju could not be reached via a foot track, this patrol was sent along Yaldor Nala to observe from the direction of Kukarthang, a ridgeline nearby.

As the patrol neared Kukarthang, heavy fire from the mountaintop made their progress impossible. The patrol leader noticed several unknown persons in black clothes hurriedly moving around on the top. With the help of his binoculars, he could also see a couple of radio antennae, a sure sign of some kind of military presence. While he was observing them, a volley of fire greeted him. He tried to disengage, but was unable to extricate the patrol, due to the heavy fire.

The commander at Batalik realized that the situation was more serious than he had thought and decided to send an officer, Captain Vikrant Avinash Desai, along with some more men to help out the patrol. Captain Desai reached the area with his party, but his efforts to link up with the patrol did not succeed as the enemy had noticed his movements too. The officer and his party found themselves out in the open with the enemy firing at them from multiple directions. They managed to take cover behind some boulders to escape the enemy's direct fire. But now it was the turn of the enemy's indirect firing weapons, the mortars, which engaged our men even behind the boulders. Luck seemed to be running out, with our team out in the open. As the freezing cold intensified, Captain Desai gathered his men

---

*A small military team sent to reconnoitre the area for any suspected enemy activities.

scattered around the boulders, and realized that he must find some cave or hideout before nightfall to ensure their safety.

Fortune favours the brave: by taking some risks, they were able to reach a rock face which, after some modifications, provided a temporary shelter from the enemy's fire and shelling. The next couple of nights passed in the biting cold, without proper extreme climate clothing.

Captain Desai, meanwhile, confirmed the presence of the enemy in the Kukarthang area to his CO, who ordered him to hold on if possible and pass on more information about the enemy. Rest or sleep remained a distant dream for the next couple of days with the enemy constantly firing at them by day as well as by night. Their rations were running out, but nothing could reach them. They ate snow or melted it to drink. Without food or water, and with no hopes of extricating himself from under the enemy's fire, Captain Vikrant Desai kept observing and continuously passing on information about whatever they gathered.

Like this, the group managed to survive for the next four days, before they could link up with Gorkha troops who had come looking for them. Under their cover, they managed to quietly slip out of this temporary base. They had spent a total of eight days in contact with the enemy.

~

While Captain Desai was observing the enemy at Kukarthang, another team was rushed from Dras to Kargil. Lieutenant Siddharth Surve, who was in charge of the team, had just joined his battalion a few months ago. He was directed to immediately reach Batalik. His team crossed a mountain pass at an altitude above 13,000 feet, at nightfall to reach there. He was further briefed at Batalik to link up with Captain Desai at Kukarthang, who was to guide him further. The officer was ordered to take up a defensive position in Yaldor Nala, up ahead of Captain Desai's location. Lt Surve travelled the whole night and reached the assigned spot by morning, ordering his men to take up positions.

They had barely found their feet when bursts of fire* greeted them, and mortar shells exploded all around them. They managed to take cover behind boulders and fired back at the enemy, who seemed to be preparing to come down on the team. Surve had orders to take up defences there, therefore, going back wasn't an option. He ordered his men to continue fighting but by midday, their ammunition ran out. His radio set also malfunctioned, cutting off communication with Captain Desai or the CO at Batalik.

Realizing the danger to his men, he ordered three out of the eight men to go back for further orders. The route was a treacherous four-hour trek, to and fro, and to hold out for this duration was almost suicidal. The brave men, however, held on for the next five hours, waiting for their colleagues to return. Just before darkness was about to fall, they heard gunshots behind them, indicating that no help was forthcoming as their colleagues had probably been ambushed by the enemy.

Lt Surve somehow managed to pull out his men after nightfall. While on his way back, he found the dead bodies of the three men he had sent lying in a pool of blood. They attempted to recover the dead bodies, but the enemy was waiting for them here too and it was the turn of another brave soldier to fall to the enemy bullets. His body was taken by Lt Surve back to the base; while those of the others were recovered much later.

~

The HQ of 3 PUNJAB were located in a flat area in the mountains in Batalik at 14,000 feet. As can be imagined, after

---

* A burst of fire is when an automatic weapon fires rapidly, discharging more than one bullet with a single press of the trigger.

the experiences of Captain Desai and Lt Surve, the activities at Batalik and Kargil were reaching a feverish pitch. Hotlines were being used to report the enemy's presence directly to Delhi. Commanders at all levels were in touch and many air-dashed to Kargil and Batalik to take stock of the situation.

As the helicopters started flying to and from Batalik on May 12, 1999, the Pakistanis saw the arrival and departure of senior army officers from across the LOC. They had missed a golden opportunity to take down the helicopters with senior officers on board. Now, they ordered their artillery to fire at Batalik Camp.

The camp was buzzing with activity with almost thirty officers present in the meeting with the Army top brass. Four officers' families were also present at the time, having arrived just a few days ago for the summer vacations. Just as the last of the helicopters flew out of Batalik, the first salvo of enemy artillery landed at the camp, missing them by only a few seconds. There was a flurry of activity with everyone running for shelter. Fortunately, two big underground shelters, called the 'Ops Room' in Army parlance, had just been prepared and were complete. All the officers and their families who were present there ran and went underground in these bunkers.

A rain of artillery shells followed the first one like a tornado, starting midday onwards. The children inside the bunkers were dazed and clung to their mothers. The shelling didn't stop till well after the fall of darkness. A few brave souls jumped out to see the damage and found that the camp was a burning inferno, with no barrack escaping extensive damage. From a distance, it resembled a mountain top that had turned into a live volcano, spewing out fire.

When they finally came out, standing amongst the remains of the buildings that had once been there, they had reasons to thank the Almighty. All the human lives had been saved. The CO immediately ordered his men to vacate the place within half an hour, but there was nowhere the enemy's artillery couldn't reach from across the LOC. The entire battalion took shelter along the road, keeping close to the shelter offered by the side of the mountain.

The officers asked their families to immediately go back to Leh and from there, to their homes. Heartrending scenes could be seen, with family members clinging to the soldiers and urging them to allow them to stay so they would all die together, if need be. The brave hearts, naturally, decided to bid farewell to their loved ones and get on with the task ahead. For Colonel Vijay Bakshi and his men, Operation Vijay had begun.

# In Neighbouring Chorbat La

Chorbat La is a mountain pass somewhere north of the Indus River and is situated on the Ladakh range near Takpochand in the northeast of the Batalik area. The Junk Lungpa and Yaldor nalas flow further west of Chorbat La. The LOC in the area generally runs southwest to northeast and takes a sharp turn outward and then inwards, forming an inverted 'V' before heading straight towards Turtok in the northeast. The area around a peak known as Gol Tekri is glaciated, making any travel extremely hazardous. There are no roads or tracks in this complete area except a cattle-grazing track connecting human settlements at Hanuthang and Handang Brok.

The area had little military presence prior to Operation Vijay, other than some Border Security Force (BSF) troops providing launchpads to occasional patrols sent from Kargil. When enemy activities on both its flanks were reported in the Turtok and Batalik-Yaldor areas, a race began to induct more troops here, in order to pre-empt the enemy and occupy the important heights all along the LOC before they could.

## Snow Tigers, Led by the Lion of Ladakh

The Ladakh Scouts, known as Snow Warriors, or Snow Tigers, for their legendary contributions, are sons of the local soil. They are familiar with the hazards and peculiarities of the mountainous terrain and, knowing the ground like the backs of their hands, are better able to navigate the harsh conditions there. Until Operation Vijay, they had mostly been used for reconnaissance missions or establishing observation posts (OPs), but were now considered most suitable for occupying fresh posts in Chorbat La.

A company of Indus Wing Ladakh Scouts was inducted to reinforce the meagre presence of our troops in the area. A strong patrol was sent to discover the extent of enemy presence in the area of Hanu Lungpa. This patrol was able to spot the enemy in the east of Junk Lungpa. The patrol leader decided to try to cut them off from the rear, but his team encountered four to five feet of waist-deep snow, forcing them to return. Subsequent patrols encountered avalanches triggered by heavy enemy artillery fire and suffered injuries when some of them were buried under the snow.

The patrols revealed that all locations except a peak known as Point 5390 were already occupied by the enemy. This peak was immediately secured the very next day. The slopes of Churubar Sispo and Bedingbar Churpo were secured within the next two days. Troops from 5 PARA also captured Point 5114, which was close to the LOC in the eastern flank of Yaldor. However, since it was now clear that the enemy was occupying much of the area west of Point 5440 along the LOC, additional troops would be needed to deal with the situation. The immediate need of the hour was to plug the gaps quickly before the enemy reached the Indus. This was planned in a unique manner: small batches of one or two soldiers were to be picked up in Cheetah helicopters and flown to the important dominating heights, along with their personal weapons. The foot columns were to link up with them subsequently.

Major Sonam Wangchuk, an officer from Ladakh, was known for his daredevil attitude despite his gentle exterior. He had studied in Solan and Dharamsala in Himachal Pradesh and at Modern School, New Delhi before getting his Bachelor's degree in History from Sri Venkateswara College of Delhi University. After his stint at the Officer Training Academy at Chennai, he had joined the Assam Regiment and had already shown his mettle in the Northeast and the Indian Peace Keeping Force in Sri Lanka. He was serving in the Ladakh Scouts and on vacation in Leh, his home town, when he was asked to re-join his unit. Before he headed to war, he sought the blessings of the Dalai Lama, who was visiting Leh at the time. He believed in his spiritual guru and had deep faith in him.

Once at the Kargil battlefront, Major Wangchuk was handpicked to go for a reconnaissance mission in the Chorbat La area along the LOC and set up an OP there. A reconnaissance mission helicopter dropped him at a place known as Gole Tekri where they were to occupy an administrative base before establishing the OP. His men were to walk up the nala and reach there by the evening. He was left with only one other soldier on an icy hilltop as the helicopter flew away. He wondered what they could do with only one rifle each and a few magazines of ammunition between them. They wouldn't last long if the enemy came! A worrying thought, but a soldier is accustomed to such uncertainties. He knew that once his men joined him, even the worst of enemies could not dislodge them. At such times, besides his training and experience in this type of tough terrain, the mental alertness of a soldier proves to be the best asset.

On 29th May, when his men arrived at nightfall, Major Wangchuk was given the firm order to capture Rock Fall, at a height of 17,500 feet. He was to soon find out that the Rock Fall area was not the innocent, scenic and snow-covered mountain top it seemed on his helicopter reconnaissance. It was glacial and rocky and extremely steep. Climbing a frozen slippery slope of eighty degrees is a tough task for even trained mountaineers, but there was no stopping this team of Snow Tigers led by Major Wangchuk.

During their advance upwards, the team came under heavy enemy fire from an ambush which had been laid to intercept them. It was not a double but triple whammy: enemy fire, the freezing cold and the steep climb on the slippery slope. One of the soldiers was fatally injured. Major Wangchuk wasted no time in asking one of the soldiers, addressed as Nunnoo (younger brother) to accompany the martyred soldier's body to the base. He then broke the ambush by charging at the enemy soldiers with his team. In the melee, the enemy lost contact with them due to their speedy movement.

The Snow Tigers continued their ascent. Despite the enemy aggressively searching for them, they managed to reach the top after another three hours of treacherous climbing under constant shelling.

At first light on 30$^{th}$ May, ten to twelve enemy soldiers were seen climbing up towards them. Major Wangchuk's team allowed the enemy to come closer and, as their heads popped up on the cliff one by one, they shot them dead with single shots from their rifles. Major Wangchuk remembered how he had wondered about the point of carrying a mere rifle at the beginning of the helicopter reconnaissance mission. In this fashion, the enemy lost seven to eight troops. However, some still hid behind boulders somewhere on the mountainside and continued to pose a deadly threat. Major Wangchuk asked Subedar Chhering Stopdon to launch an attack on them with the troops under his command. This was the last straw for the enemy soldiers, who fled. Rock Fall was in our hands.

This was the first victory of the war in Kargil. Not only did it boost the morale of the soldiers at the front, it sent home the message that it was only a matter of time before the Pakistani intruders would be thrown back. Also, it was here that first-hand evidence of Pakistan's involvement was obtained, as the bodies of the enemy soldiers were recovered in the follow-up action, along with their weapons. They were identified as soldiers of the Northern Light Infantry which forms a part of the regular army in Pakistan. Initially, during those days, Pakistan officially denied its involvement and, in fact, shamefully claimed that these men were militants who were not under its control. It refused to take the bodies of the soldiers who died during this action, until much later, around June, by when media pressure had built up and could not be ignored.

For their feats of daring bravery, Major Sonam Wangchuk was awarded the Maha Vir Chakra, and Subedar Chhering Stopdan the Vir Chakra. Today, Colonel Sonam Wangchuk is known as the Lion of Ladakh; an apt name for the legendary man.

~

Within the next couple of days, the high positions of Chorbat La near the LOC were occupied by Indian troops. However, the area westward of Point 5440 remained with the Pakistanis till later. By early June, three more companies of Ladakh Scouts were inducted and placed under the command of Karakoram Wing. However, due to the high concentration of enemy forces opposite this area, they were later replaced with regular troops from the 14th Battalion of the Sikh Regiment (14 SIKH).

By mid-June, the Ladakh Scouts established a link with the troops coming up from the Yaldor Nala, and the regular forces confirmed that there was no enemy presence at Gonpa Thang ridgeline, thus effectively sealing any further intrusion into the area.

# Further North-East in Turtok

East of the Ladakh Range, the area up to the Southern Siachen Glacier is barren, with only a few villages dotting this frozen landscape. Prominent amongst them are Turtok and Tyakshi. This area was recaptured by the Indian Army in 1971, when Lt Col Rinchen had freed the locals from Pakistan's earlier annexation of their land. By 1999, Pakistan once again harboured designs for a major offensive in this area.

At the end of April and in early May, Indian soldiers on the isolated icy posts along the LOC had noticed several Pakistani helicopters carrying loads slung under the bodies of the choppers. To confirm the nature of the Pakistani activities, a patrol of the Jat Regiment was sent to this area. As the patrol drew closer to the LOC in these uninhabited and inaccessible glaciated mountains, they drew enemy fire and lost one of their members. Another patrol was sent out, but could not access the area due to bad weather. Subsequently, a large number of patrols were sent to find out exactly what was happening along the LOC. Their reports confirmed that Pakistan had occupied many peaks and ridges at several spots in the area.

Until then, Indian and Pakistani troops had faced each other across the LOC only up to a place popularly known as Vee Gap. South of this line, the entire area is very precipitous and glaciated almost up to Chorbat La, and was not actively occupied by either side. Keeping in mind the reports of enemy activity developing in other sectors, reinforcements were required to hold these heights and prevent any intrusion by Pakistani forces. Some of our troops already present in the area were hurriedly diverted and rushed through Turtok to prevent the enemy's ingress. There were no roads or tracks in the area, and they needed the skill of expert mountaineers to scale peak after peak. Without fearing what lay ahead, the Indian Army marched on and, by mid-May, most of the columns had reached near the LOC.

## Haneef's Call

It was the early days in Kargil war, not much information about the enemy intrusion was known. One of the companies of 11 RAJ RIF was deployed in Turtok region. Lt Haneefuddin was one of the officers posted in the company. As part of the operations of the battalion to secure all possible vulnerable areas, he was the first to attempt to capture Point 5590 in Turtok. Haneef belonged to Delhi and had studied at Shivaji College. He was a very talented student and was crowned 'Mr Shivaji' in his college days. His talents endeared him to his troops as well.

On 6th June, Lt Haneefuddin commenced his maiden attempt. Suddenly, bullets started whizzing past him and his small team consisting of three men. Unfazed by the enemy fire, this brave soldier continued to climb down from a height nearby towards this peak, when he was hit by a bullet which made him lose his balance. He fell deep into a crack in the glacier along with another soldier, Naib Subedar Mangez Singh from his team. As the glacier was on the Pakistani side of the LOC, his body could not be recovered immediately. Clouds descended from the mountain top and covered his body as if preparing to take him to the heavens.

Lt Haneefuddin's death came as a blow, not only to his colleagues, but also the entire nation, who immortalized him by renaming part of this place as Sub-sector Haneef, SSH for short.

Haneef's father had passed away when he was a child. His

mother, Hema Aziz was a proud woman who didn't believe in pity and charities. In a conversation with the journalist Rachna Bisht she said, 'Haneef was a soldier and was doing his duty towards his nation. I would not have expected him to turn back to save his life.'

Haneef was honoured with the Vir Chakra on the following Independence Day.

Point 5590 was finally recaptured by Lt Haneef's battalion a month later, thereby avenging his death. When the Army Chief General V.P. Malik had told Hema Aziz that his body could not be retrieved for more than forty days because the enemy was firing constantly, she had replied, 'I do not want another soldier to risk his life to get my son's body.'

~

Pakistan's sinister designs in launching a major offensive in Turtok area was now amply clear. Hundreds of blasts had been heard at the beginning of the summer months, which suggested that a road was being constructed in the Mian Lungpa area. The capture of five suspects in Turtok, around the same time as when the Kargil intrusion was detected, had led to the apprehension of another two dozen suspects in three villages nearby, with a large amount of arms and ammunition. The villagers had been wary of their presence for some time, but had not mustered the courage to inform the nearby military post, fearing reprisals. These suspects spilled the beans and divulged Pakistan's plans to generate militancy in order to support its attack across the LOC. It had aimed to capture Turtok and Chalunka, an area forming the rear of the Siachen Glacier. There were indications that Pakistan had constructed several helipads and had a huge tented campus which could harbour thousands of soldiers on its own side of the LOC. Pakistani plans had suffered a severe blow by the timely reaction of our forces and the brave acts of men like Haneefuddin.

# Intrusion in Kaksar
## In the Shadow of Kargil

The Kaksar area overlooks National Highway 1D, just short of Kargil. The 4$^{th}$ Battalion of the Jat Regiment (4 JAT) was in charge of the area. On 14 May 1999, they sent a patrol under Lt Saurabh Kalia up to Bajrang Post, which was a part of their defences, but was usually left vacant during the winter.

Lt Kalia was asked to check whether it was indeed clear of the enemy or not. Six brave men accompanied him. The glaciated nature of the region did not allow rapid movement, but they made their way towards it steadily, through the knee-deep snow. The approach to the post was comparatively easier from the Pakistani side; the enemy had taken full advantage of this over the winter and by then had occupied it. Captain Kalia's patrol had barely reached the Bajrang Post from the south when Pakistani soldiers appeared out of nowhere and surrounded them. They were all taken as Prisoners of War.

By nightfall, the battalion was worried as they hadn't heard from Lt Kalia. The officiating CO sent a search party, under Lt Amit Bharadwaj, to the same area. On reaching the Bajrang Post's southern approach, this patrol, too, came under heavy fire. The enemy was waiting for them with their weapons ready and the patrol was out in the open, an easy target.

Almost everyone in the patrol was injured and Lt Bharadwaj

was seriously wounded. Despite his injuries, he ordered his men to clear out from the area, while he, along with Havildar Rajbir Singh, held onto the enemy. There was no further communication from them. The two brave companions must have fought till they breathed their last, judging from the postures of their frozen, maggot-infested bodies which could only be recovered after the cease-fire that came into effect in July 1999.

The mutilated bodies of Lt Saurabh Kalia and his men were finally handed over by Pakistan on 9th June. Some time previously, an unidentified Pakistani radio call had been intercepted; while abusing the Indian Army at a post close to the LOC known as Bimbat LC, the enemy soldier had boasted that Lt Kalia was being ordered to cook and wash utensils in captivity, and being stabbed repeatedly to comply. Lt Saurabh Kalia chose rather to die for his motherland.

The mutilation of the dead bodies returned by Pakistan exposed its insensitivity to human values and shocked not only India, but also the world. It strengthened India's resolve, more than ever before. No one could beat the spirit of the awakened giant now. It was only a matter of time before sheer will-power and bravery would throw the enemy out. Kargil became a rallying point, and everyone now wanted to do their bit. Of the hundreds and thousands of letters of encouragement and resolution which were sent to the troops, one which stirred the soul was that of a young girl who wrote with her own blood, saying, 'Although my frail body would not allow me to fight at such altitudes, I may be cut into pieces, tied to explosives and thrown on the path of the Pakistanis.'

# West of Kargil
## Dras–Mashkoh

Dras is situated along National Highway 1D at a distance of approximately 200 kilometres from Srinagar. It is the coldest inhabited place in the world: the temperature habitually falls to minus sixty degrees Celsius during the winter. Due to the heavy snow, the pass on the highway, Zoji La, closes between October and May every year, making travel impossible during those months.

Mashkoh Valley lies to the northwest of Dras, and joins the Kishan-Ganga Valley to the north of Zoji La. Most of the area north of Mashkoh Nala is glaciated. There are no navigable tracks in this area, except one along the Mashkoh Nala, which traditionally served the inhabitants of Mashkoh Valley. A similar track along the Bimbat Nala towards the LOC also served as a traditional route for locals. In the pre-Partition days, a track also used to lead to the Marpo La pass to the north of Dras.

Dras is overlooked by a ridgeline which cuts across the LOC near Point 5353 and runs up to Point 4700. Another ridgeline east of the ridge terminates at Tololing, short of Dras. Tiger Hill, although not the highest feature, dominates most of the area around Dras. Its peculiar shape resembles the head of a tiger, but it also takes its name from the snow leopards that once inhabited this place. North of Tiger Hill, the area is glaciated and there is a small frozen lake called Pariyon ka Talab, which features in folklore as a place for fairies to frolic.

Dras-Mashkoh was looked after by an infantry battalion, the 16 Grenadiers (16 GREN). The movement of enemy soldiers across the LOC towards Dras was possible only through the gaps at Marpo La and Bimbat Nala. A company had blocked each of these gaps and the balance troops had formed reserves, which could be moved towards either Kargil or Mashkoh as required. Although some troops were deployed along the Mashkoh Nala to prevent infiltration during the summer, there was no army presence over the winter. Typically, all the hill features in this area would have remained unoccupied after the passes closed, as staying on the ridgelines for long durations is not feasible without a supply of fresh and dry rations. Instead, occasional patrols were sent to check out any activities that may have taken place during the winter, and planned aerial surveillance sorties by the Air Force maintained a close watch on the ridgelines and the gaps in between.

In the first week of May 1999, a Ladakh Scout patrol of Bimbat Nala was on its routine patrol towards the LOC in Dras when they noticed some movement on a peak north of Tololing. There appeared to be a couple of men moving around on the top. This report, sent on 12$^{th}$ May, in conjunction with the action already taking place in the Batalik-Yaldor-Chorbat La area and beyond, confirmed the fears of enemy presence in Dras. A helicopter surveillance mission noticed alarming movements, with men spotted in several places on the ridgeline ending at Tololing. By 13$^{th}$ May it was confirmed they were the enemy.

A flurry of activity began: phones buzzed, faxes shot back and forth, radio sets exchanged urgent messages, and orders started pouring in, one after another... It was clear that NH 1D was under enemy threat. The enemy's exact location was not clear, but it was assessed that they were occupying the ridgelines leading right up to Dras. They would be able to dominate and

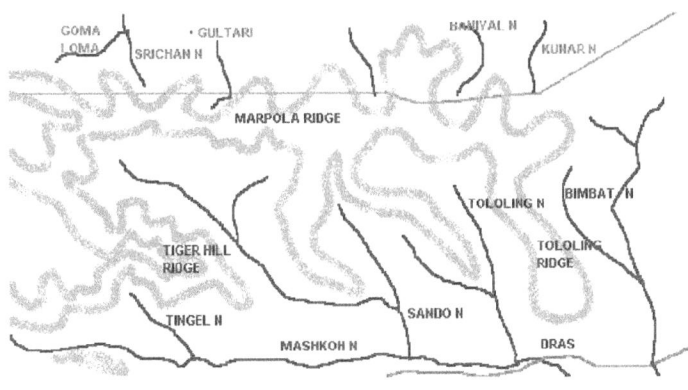

MAP 3: Dras Area

cut off the highway, and wouldn't allow any movement on it. A grim situation!

At the time, a single battalion was already deployed in Sando and Bimbat Nala. Another battalion was just rolling in from Srinagar, on their way to Batalik. As they thought of calling it a day before it got completely dark and started parking their vehicles, the enemy greeted them with a volley of heavy artillery fire; the first of many shellings in Dras.

This battalion, none other than the First Battalion of the Naga Regiment (1 NAGA), was under the command of Major P.K. Sharma. He rallied his troops and quickly moved them to a safer place nearby. They were briefed by the Kargil Brigade Commander about the presence of the enemy on the ridgelines in Dras. 1 NAGA was asked to clear the heights in Dras overlooking the highway as quickly as possible—it was expected that they would take approximately five or six days to completely clear it.

One of the first planning parameters is to know who and where the enemy is, and in what strength. There was no time to find this out. The information available to them for assessment suggested that only a few militants were hiding on the hilltops. They assumed that they would only need a few platoons to eliminate them, or chase them away from the area. A plan was made and approved by the next morning.

The plan involved using three of their companies as a left hook through the Sando Nala. These companies were to go deep towards the LOC and start clearing the intruders from their rear at Point 5100, a height close to the LOC on the Marpo La Ridgeline. The battalion was to then come back, rolling the enemy down from there along the ridgeline and link up at Point 5140 (close to the highway) with their right hook, which would be advancing along the Bimbat Nala. It seemed to be a good plan to hit the enemy from the rear and front simultaneously. But sometimes the best plans go horrendously wrong, due to lack of time and wrong assessment. Only time would tell what lay ahead.

# Part II

# Initial Battles

# Igloos Save the Day

1 NAGA started their operational march on the night of 15th May, towards Sando, a steady 10-kilometre climb. Tiger Hill overlooks this entire area. By early morning the next day, they had reached Sando Post and, after a short halt, began to move towards Point 5100 through the Gorkha Nala. As the day broke, the first artillery shell landed close to this attacking column. By the time they could react and find cover, the second and third bombs had fallen right in front of them in the Gorkha Nala. This forced them to halt.

A rain of artillery fire delayed their advance by a couple of hours. Surprisingly, it was seemingly controlled at Tiger Hill; so far, the enemy had not been seen there. The Nagas managed to survive this onslaught, too, and resumed their advance by evening.

By early next morning, the leading company under Captain Ved Pal Yadav was able to reach close to the top, a height of more than 15,000 feet. There was snow all around them and the temperature was way below freezing point. The ferocity of the cold wind cut through their winter clothing. It was if they had landed at the North Pole straight from the green and beautiful Kashmir valley!

The passage got narrower thereafter and only a few men could move ahead at a time. No longer a march, they had to climb on all fours as the snow was slippery and difficult to negotiate. The weapons hanging from their shoulders didn't make it any easier. No sooner had the leading men reached a few metres short of the ridgeline than machine guns suddenly started spitting fire from the top!

Our soldiers were quick to take cover after the first volley hit the snow nearby. However, in their rush for cover, they slipped down the hill to the starting point! To fire uphill upon the enemy was not possible. Therefore, two small teams were split off and tasked with reaching the top.

Daylight soon broke and there was no place to hide. The enemy could easily see them against the white background of the snow and pick them off, one by one. A quick solution was needed. Soldiers are conditioned to think on their feet, and someone remembered their school lessons on the Inuit tribes, who used to live in igloos in the Arctic Circle. Igloos are snow houses or snow huts—shelters built from snow when it is easy to compact. Well, they were in similar conditions here, so why not do the same? It was a good idea—worth a try, especially as time was running out. They dug into the snow, and each one created a burrow, forming an igloo dome over it, and slid into it to conceal themselves from the enemy. These igloos saved the day for them.

Over the course of the day, they observed that the enemy was reinforcing the positions at the top and would be ready to receive them, if they managed to climb. Night fell. Once again, five teams were sent to reach the ridgeline, but heavy enemy fire thwarted them. The worst was when the enemy started to roll boulders and stones down from the top, knocking down anyone in their path and hitting the Gorkha Nala below with loud thuds. Fortunately, the Nagas had had the good sense to make their igloos in such places where the rolling boulders passed over them and went harmlessly down the slope.

A stalemate had developed. Therefore, one of the companies was asked to remain on the mountainside, while the others were asked to come down and reinforce their eastern hook developing through Bimbat Nala. The company remained in the igloos above Gorkha Nala for the next couple of days under the command of Major Madan. Food would be delivered only once in twenty-four hours, and always at night. The khichdi, shakkarparas or pooris sent by the Sando post were accompanied with melted snow! Since even that invited enemy fire, the rations of melted snow also had to be restricted. The men braved it out in these nerve-wracking conditions for almost ten days before being asked to return to the base and re-join the battalion.

Fortunately, no lives were lost during this entire operation. Point 5100 still stood there, as a challenge to be overcome later (See Map 7).

# Hotel on the Top
## Point 5140

On the eastern flank, a company of 1 NAGA commanded by Major Shalabh Tripathi, was ordered to move along the Bimbat Nala and capture Point 5140. An old track that led from Bimbat village near Dras to Marpho La Pass on the LOC at a height of approximately 15,000 feet used to be an additional route in the past, connecting Kargil to Kunar (presently in POK). However, it was in a state of disuse when the company decided to follow it. Starting from the highway, the ground gradually slopes upwards, until Tololing peak is crossed to one's left side. The track becomes steeper thereafter and Point 5140 comes into view behind Tololing. In the mountains, the tracks often cross over rivers or nalas, and wooden bridges are used wherever possible.

On 15th May, when the company reached a wooden bridge on the Bimbat Nala, the enemy was positioned on the ridgeline emanating from Point 5140, and opened fire with their machine guns. They fired parachuting illumination flares to detect the company's movements and, to make matters worse, soon artillery shells started hitting the ground nearby. Regardless, Major Tripathi ordered his men to take cover and move on. They managed to reach a place referred to as 'Administration Base', which was earlier established to trans-ship the logistic loads for troops deployed on the posts at LOC. After a short halt, this team continued advancing ahead towards the rear of Point 5140, to first cut the enemy off from his supplies from the LOC side before attacking them (See Map 7).

A night halt was required. A nearby place was marked with an 'H' in a circle on the map. A message was passed on the radio set to the battalion HQ that their halt would be taken at Hotel. Who gave this name and why? The answer lies in the practice of marking a helipad as 'H' on the map, combined with the signalling format by which the letter 'H' is generally read as Hotel for clarity when communicating on radio. Whatever it might be, it became a place to rest high up in the mountains, although their beds were made of snow, and bone-chilling winds provided the lulling music.

From Hotel, there was a sharp ridgeline running for almost one kilometre to Point 5140. The snow on top of this ridgeline had hardened, and any movement along this ridge needed special mountaineering skills. Major Tripathi had not learnt to give up and decided to carry on with his reconnaissance, early the next day. Barely had he covered half the distance to Point 5140, when all hell broke loose. Bullets flew all around him. He saw one of his men fatally shot, and two others injured. Before long, three enemy bullets found their way into his shoulders and collarbone as well, and he needed immediate medical attention.

To retrieve these injured men from under enemy fire from the ridgeline was a Himalayan adventure worthy of only the bravest. To bring an injured soldier on a stretcher requires a minimum of four people and, usually, another four to relieve them every fifteen minutes due to breathing difficulties in high altitudes. Major Tripathi and the others were brought down after an arduous attempt lasting ten hours.

Night fell, and further evacuation by helicopter was not possible until dawn. A helicopter managed to reach them the next day and brought the injured to the safety of the nearest ad-hoc Army hospital. The Hotel location continued to be occupied by the rest of the company. Captain N. Ashok was now ordered to take over command of this company and was moved from Gorkha Nala to the Hotel.

For the next couple of days, Captain Ashok continued probing towards Point 5140, but in vain. During the day, movement along the ridgeline could be spotted by the enemy. The hours of darkness were limited, as day broke early on those heights. Progress was rather slow. However, Captain Ashok was not disheartened, and continued to advance. His experience with the igloos allowed him to take cover during halts till it was time to move on again. By the end of the second week, he was only a few hundred metres away from Point 5140.

However, a major obstacle had to be surmounted: a huge rock face jutted out upwards and there seemed to be no way to cross it. Captain Ashok deployed his machine gun and started to explore a way to advance over the rock face. It was midday when an enemy bunker near Point 5140 opened up with machine guns at him. The bullets hit his radio operator who died on the spot, leaving a damaged radio set and disrupting communications with the base. The rest of the Naga battalion at Administration Base in Bimbat Nala could only hear the heavy firing taking place on top.

The fate of Captain Ashok and his team was not known till a messenger sent down by him conveyed that although he had been hit by rocket splinters in his liver, thigh and one eye, he was, nevertheless, stable!

Lance Naik Khusimun Gurung was one of the troops who fought there at Hotel with Captain Ashok. He not only seemed bold and energetic, but displayed his bravery and tenacity in abundance when the time came. He continuously engaged the enemy with his machine gun, despite grave risk to himself. He didn't take any rest and continued to assist in moving casualties to a place of greater safety, from where they were subsequently evacuated to a safe place. He was awarded the Vir Chakra later for his determination and outstanding bravery, despite grave risks to his own safety.

CO 1 NAGA discussed the above situation with his superiors and took a call to disengage from this direction too and asked the company to fall back halfway, and stay put.

The administration chain had nearly collapsed after fighting for almost twenty days. By now, the operation had already taken a toll of four lives, and injured sixteen more. The weather had also affected the fitness levels of the officers. In the first week of June, it was decided that the Naga battalion be pulled back to 'Rest and Refit' for two weeks. A battalion of the Grenadier Regiment took over the area thereafter.

# The Crawlers of Tiger Hill

On 12$^{th}$ May, closely following the Naga battalion, the 8$^{th}$ Battalion of the Sikh Regiment (8 SIKH) under their CO, Colonel S.P. Singh, had crossed over Zoji La. Heavy artillery shelling greeted them too, and the battalion could not advance beyond Pandras. The CO, however, managed to reach Dras despite enemy shelling. He was briefed about the situation and told to send one company to the Brigade HQ for a special mission immediately on the next day.

Only scanty information about the enemy was available and the local commander had thought that there were only a few militants hiding in the area. He had planned a special mission to surround Tiger Hill from all the directions by splitting this company into eight to nine small teams. Tiger Hill is an imposing height with a clear view of Dras and part of Mashkoh valley and is located away from the highway, but close to the LOC. Sando Nala separates it from the ridgeline emanating from Marpo La ridge which terminates at Tololing, near Dras.

The rest of the battalion had orders, after they had arrived at Dras, to move to Tiger Hill and join up and strengthen the company that had already been sent to Brigade HQ in advance on a special mission. It was expected that the militants would not offer much resistance and the area would be clear without a big fight. But this was not to be!

The CO of 8 SIKH had realized that it would be difficult to have command and control over so many small teams after the troops were split up. If this plan was to be adopted, additional detail to its logistics was also urgently needed, as well as extra equipment, like radio sets. Therefore, he modified the plan after discussing it with his brigade commander. The company was asked to move through the Tingle Nala, which is on the west of Tiger Hill towards Mashkoh, and secure Point 4460 and Point 4195 south of Tiger Hill on the ridgeline. It was here that the enemy had been seen by 16 GREN's patrols a few days back. 16 GREN had been the only battalion operating in this huge tract of land for some time now and had occupied the defences over a large area (See p. 38).

~

Before the Sikh battalion finally reached Dras on 14th May, Major Saxena's company had already been launched on a special mission and was progressing towards Point 4460. This column was successful in occupying Point 4460. The rest of the battalion commenced movement the next day. By the next evening, there had been a fresh sighting of enemy movement in Mashkoh Valley and the plan was re-made. The battalion was tasked with surrounding Tiger Hill from all directions and isolating it.

The men of the Sikh Regiment, known as the Khalsas, moved up the Dras-Sando track and reached Sando Post. The Naga battalion had passed through the same place earlier and had got stuck in the Gorkha Nala thereafter.

Colonel S.P. Singh led the unit from the front and began the steep climb towards the top of Tiger Hill. To conceal their actions from direct observation by the enemy, they moved at night. By the morning, the column was able to reach Point 4460 from the eastern side of Tiger Hill via Sando Nala and link up with Major Saxena's company, who had earlier reached the location. However, when the day broke, the company following the CO's party had not yet closed in. The rest of the group took a short halt and, just when they seemed to be settling down, a few

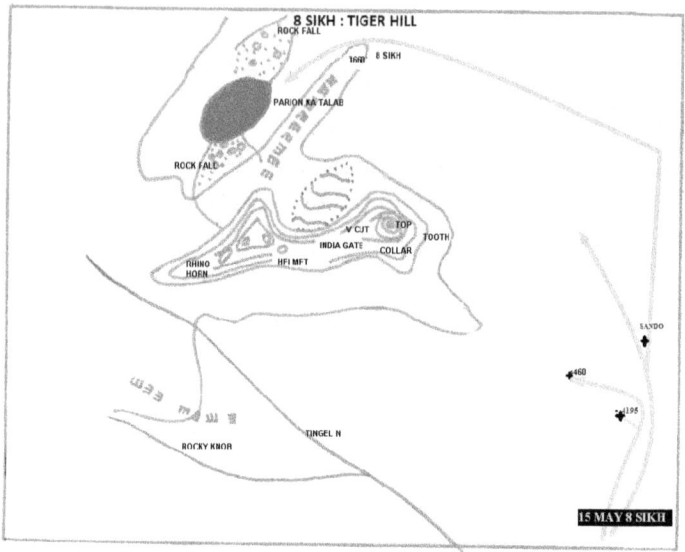

MAP 4: Initial Isolation of Tiger Hill

enemy soldiers sprang out of their hide-outs and sprayed bullets randomly, killing two, including a JCO, on the spot and injuring sixteen others.

The Sikhs retaliated furiously. A heavy exchange of fire lasted the entire day. However, since the enemy occupied the higher features, they were in a position of advantage where they could prevent the the evacuation of our casualties. Our infantry mortars were brought up to keep the enemy's head down while the casualties were being evacuated down to Sando Post by night. When the injured passed through the CO's location, they opened their eyes and murmured, 'Assi theek haan!' ('We are fine!').

By the following midday, the Sikh battalion was asked to redirect one of its companies to the west of Tiger Hill, via Parion-ka-Talab. Delta Company was given this arduous task. It started immediately, without any rest, and reached Parion-ka-Talab by the next morning. The remaining battalion continued to divert the enemy from the Sando Post. Delta Company was now supposed to probe forward towards Shivling area near the end of the western spur* of Tiger Hill. The complete area was covered with heavy snow and the company had to cross a glacier before reaching the base of Shivling. They reached the spot by the following midday, and now, their movement became quite slow. This was precisely the opportunity the enemy at Tiger Hill was waiting for.

Firing started from all directions. The company returned fire, but the enemy was well entrenched on higher ground on all sides. By evening, most of the soldiers had had to extricate themselves to safer positions. A head count revealed that five, including Lt Kanad Bhattacharya, had gone missing or dead. Sixteen others were injured during this encounter. However, no dead bodies could be recovered due to the enemy's heavy fire.

The company was now beefed up by pulling out some men from the battalion headquarters, and Major Dalbir took control of the operations. More than ten continuous fighting days had passed, but the company once again marched up, with the multiple aims of recovering their dead, clearing the Shivling area and dislodging the enemy bases on the ridgelines. They were able to recover three dead bodies, but Lt Kanad Bhattacharya and one more soldier's whereabouts were still not traceable. Once again, their movement seemed to have been detected by the enemy. Moreover, heavy automatics, rockets and artillery fire made any progress impossible. They had to return to the base before daybreak.

~

Delta Company was now asked to change the route and climb up towards Tiger Hill near a place known as Junction Point, and

---

* A lateral ridge descending from a hill, mountain or the main crest of a ridge.

progress towards Shivling from there, instead of heading straight upwards to the enemy held height. The company succeeded in reaching the ridgeline near Junction Point. Progress was very slow, though, and they could only inch forward towards Shivling.

In the meanwhile, the company at Sando Post was tasked to move ahead and occupy Point 4460. The company that had arrived there earlier was relieved to tackle operations to capture Tiger Hill. By 21$^{st}$ May, the Khalsas were everywhere around Tiger Hill, except the western side. Every night, trenches would be dug, to dive into when the enemy fired. They would then move upwards a bit, and repeat the procedure, thus crawling inch by inch to the top. The enemy kept firing with automatics and artillery continuously onto this adamant company of the Sikhs that refused to give up. The stalemate was to continue for some time to come.

# Warriors of the Mist

The Sikhs were followed by the 18th Battalion of the Grenadiers Regiment (18 GREN), the same group that had raced under their Commanding Officer, Colonel Khushal Thakur, to cross Zoji La at the earliest and reach Mughalpura by 17th May. This unit[*] is known as the 'Pole Star Battalion', for its steadfastness in the battlefield. The time had come for them to prove themselves worthy of this title yet again.

The change from the beautiful Kashmir Valley to the barren and snowy heights of the Great Himalayan Range requires acclimatization so that the body gets accustomed to the rarefied oxygen at these altitudes. The battalion took no time to switch over to the new surroundings and was ready to launch its first attack on Tololing heights by the fifth day. Mist had enveloped the mountains and an eerie silence prevailed.

Tololing overlooks Dras and a large section of the National Highway. Point 4590 is another feature to the southwest of Tololing towards the highway. Any movement on the highway in Dras was not safe until both Tololing and Point 4590 were clear of the enemy. There were only two alternatives possible to reach the top of Tololing. One possibility was to go around and approach from the steep northern route, while the second was to climb up straight from the south, where there was a slightly more gradual slope. The northern approach to Tololing was full of

---

[*] Unit or paltan are alternative names for any battalion in the Indian Army.

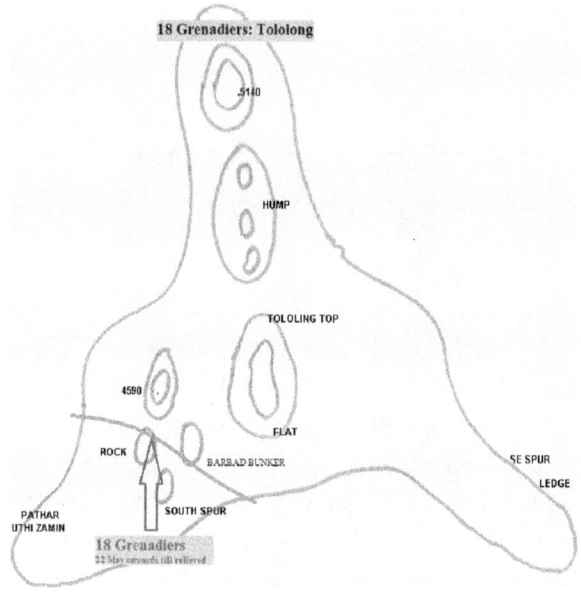

MAP 5: Tololing

snow and rocky outcrops, so the most obvious frontal approach from the south and southwest had to be adopted by 18 GREN.

16 GREN, who were already in contact with the enemy in this area, were to provide the firm base from where 18 GREN were to be securely launched. 1 NAGA was to attack Point 5140 and support this operation by dividing the enemy's reaction.

On the night of 22nd May, the D-day for 18 GREN to launch their attack on Tololing, Alpha Company, under Major Randhir Singh Rathor, led the battalion to first secure Point 4590, before closing in towards Tololing. It was a foggy night with the temperature dipping towards freezing point. The Ghataks, or commando teams under Lt Balwan and Captain Sachin Nimbalkar were scouting ahead. As the company almost covered the entire bad stretch upwards, and were within a 1000 metres of Tololing, the weather started packing up. Before anyone could realize it, there was rain and snow. A pretty sight, under different circumstances, but now they were facing a steep, slippery climb!

The enemy waited until the company reached striking distance. Daylight had broken out by then, rendering them all the more vulnerable. Suddenly, all hell broke loose. The automatic and artillery fire seemed to be coming from all sides. The firefight continued for the next two days, without either of the parties giving up. One of the leading men in the company was fatally wounded. Alpha Company seemed to have no option but to pull back to get out of the enemy's range, but decided to remain there itself.

The troops from 16 GREN had also advanced very close to Point 4590, but they couldn't hold it. They had to fall back, as they were in open terrain without any big boulders to take cover behind.

Meanwhile, Bravo Company under Major Rajesh Adhikari climbed up the south spur to the left of Alpha Company, while Charlie Company under Joy Dasgupta, and Delta Company under Major Vishal, approached from even further left on the western spur. These companies on the western spur came under heavy fire from Tololing and Point 5140 where the enemy's machine guns were sighted.

Bravo Company managed to reach just short of a place called Barbad Bunker, at Tololing Top. Once again, a firefight broke out. To make matters worse, one of the medium machine guns (MMGs) broke down and needed urgent replacement. Another MMG was quickly rushed to the spot, but by the time it reached them, the sun was ready to shine! The company had lost a few men already, so they, too, were asked to consolidate their position.

An intermittent rain of artillery and automatic fire continued for the next couple of days, allowing neither of the parties to rest or recoup. To soften up the target area before a further attack, the Air Force was requested to take the enemy on. Major Rajesh Adhikari was asked to go back down to guide the helicopters and show them where to shoot.

On 28th May, the operations began with MI-17 helicopters moving in to destroy the enemy bunkers on Tololing Top. The enemy had managed to sneak in a few missiles, which were fired at these helicopter sorties. Due to evasive action taken by the helicopters, they were successful the first three times in causing damage to the enemy bunkers; however, the fourth helicopter was not so lucky. One of the missiles found its way accurately, and the unfortunate helicopter slowly sank towards the ground, before exploding in mid-air, killing all on board.

Tololing stood there, mocking all efforts and demanding more bloodshed in the days to come. This first attack on Tololing had allowed the army to have a more accurate assessment of the enemy's defences and deployment, and so the approach plan needed some adjustments. By then, additional artillery was also available to support the assault. While tons of ammunition—rocket launchers, mortars, machine guns and grenade launchers—were lugged up to replenish the company before the next assault, the enemy continued to fire relentlessly from Tololing. Their line of supply seemed to be still intact. The second attack on Tololing by 18 GREN was launched on the night of 29th May.

Major Rajesh Adhikari was assigned to capture the Barbad Bunker. He was a Mechanized Infantry Officer[*] on cross attachment[†] with the battalion. Known as 'Addy' to his close friends, he was a highlander from Nainital, and loved the mountains. He was well known for his physical toughness and a commando-like approach to life, but beneath this hard exterior he loved to play guitar and sing. He often sang 'Tears in Heaven' and 'Everything I Do', along with other songs by his favourite

---

[*] Mechanized Infantry are equipped with armoured personnel carriers (APCs) or infantry-fighting vehicles (IFVs) for transport and combat.

[†] An officer can stay and fight with a supporting arm (e.g. ASC with Infantry battalion) for a specific a period before reverting back to parent regiment.

singers: Eric Clapton, Cliff Richards and Bryan Adams. Addy was looking forward to celebrating his first wedding anniversary with his college sweetheart on 9$^{th}$ June, merely ten days away at the time of his assignment to Barbad Bunker.

As the attack began again, bullets and artillery shells continued to explode all around them. Addy did not flinch but advanced steadily, unfazed by the heavy firing. Inching steadily, he was a few metres short of the Barbad Bunker at past midnight when a burst of bullets tore through him, killing him on the spot. His radio operator was injured as well, but he continued to pass on a minute-by-minute report on the progress of the operations. With a choked voice, he conveyed the martyrdom of his company commander to the CO.

'Tears in Heaven' rang in the hearts of his colleagues as they bade adieu to this brave Warrior of the Mist. Major Rajesh Adhikari was awarded a Maha Vir Chakra posthumously for his outstanding bravery. His body could only be recovered by the next battalion in a subsequent attack. Instead of an anniversary gift, his wife received the tricolour wrapped body of a martyr. In his pocket lay her unopened letter, which he had not had time to read ever since he received it when he came down to the base to guide the Air Force helicopters.

~

Heavens may shed tears, but soldiers are made of sterner stuff. They know that the real tribute to a martyr lies in contributing to the cause for which he laid down his life. Although by now there were two fatal casualties and eight injured soldiers, the Grenadiers didn't want to stop. They consolidated themselves and collected warriors who would do or die for the same cause. There was no dearth of volunteers who wished to avenge the death of their comrades at Tololing. On the night of 2$^{nd}$ June, Lt Col R. Vishwanathan, Vishu to his friends, led the team and

Colonel Khushal Thakur, the CO, followed him, on their third attempt to capture Tololing.

The moon had risen high above in the sky by the time they found themselves almost at an arm's length from the by-now-infamous Barbad Bunker. Lance Havildar Ram Kumar was immediately ahead, leading the assault. He engaged the enemy bunker, but in the melee, faced a burst of machine gun fire to his chest. Despite bleeding profusely, he rose like a phoenix and lobbed a hand grenade into the bunker, killing a few of the enemy inside. They ran out of the bunker, only to find Lance Havildar Ram Kumar staring at them with his rifle ready to fire. He killed two more before finally collapsing to the ground.

Bullets flew and artillery shells exploded all around, and the resultant smoke masked the moonlight. As Vishu found himself pinned to the ground, he asked for our own fire to stop, so that he could crawl up to the Bunker and destroy it. The CO looked back to give clearance through his radio set, but found no one behind him. His radio operator had been shot dead!

A few seconds later, he heard Vishu's radio operator shouting to him that Vishu had been badly wounded. The CO rushed forward and found him in a pool of blood, mumbling incoherently. He had been injured in the thigh and the groin. Six valiant soldiers lay dead close to him.

Vishu refused to be evacuated, knowing that he was beyond recovery, and asked his CO to take other injured casualties down and save their lives as he would ultimately succumb to his injuries. The CO evacuated him speedily despite his protests, but yet another Warrior of the Mist became a martyr before reaching the base at Tololing.

Lt Col R. Vishwanathan and Lance Havildar Ram Kumar were awarded Vir Chakras for their outstanding bravery in this operation.[*] But how much bloodshed did Tololing still need?

---

[*] Bammi, Lt. Gen. Y.M., (Retd), *Kargil*, p. 209.

# Part III

# Victories Begin

# Turning the Tide in Dras

## An Indian Tsunami at Tololing

The deepest penetration beyond the LOC by the intruders in Dras was up to Tololing Heights. They stayed put there and didn't open fire until they were detected on 12th May 1999. They used this time to create their defensive infrastructure in such a manner that any movement towards their location would be met with tremendous firepower. 18 Grenadiers, who had been there for almost two weeks now, were only able to encircle them, and their ring still had a gap in the direction of Point 5140.

The 2nd Battalion of the Rajputana Rifles (2 RAJ RIF) regiment was operating in the Valley after having undergone extensive training at the Corps Battle School in Khrew. They got the warning order to move to Sonmarg on 25th May. The unit took no time to prepare and move to Sonmarg, ultimately reaching Dras on 1st June.

The battalion was initially tasked with capturing Hump, behind Tololing, but later their objective was changed to Tololing itself. The aim was to ensure that the gains made by the Grenadiers were further exploited.

From the battle held at Tololing so far, it was clear that the enemy was occupying it in strength, and not in penny packets as had been assessed earlier. It was also evident that not only did the enemy hold the Tololing Top and Point 5140, but the entire ridgeline, including Hump and Rocky Knob, in between these

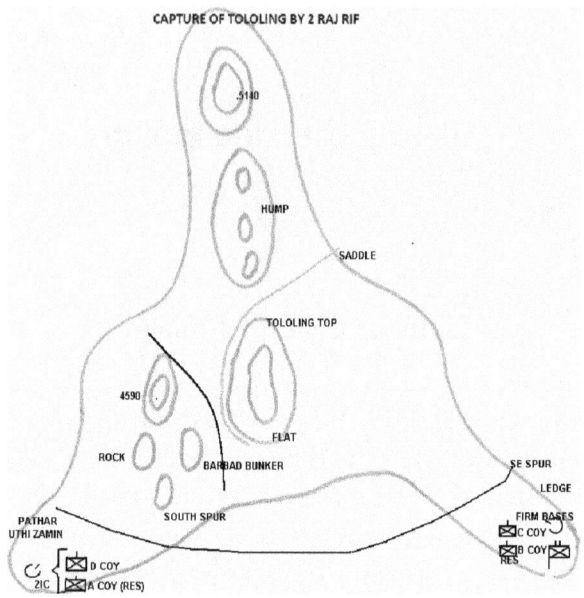

MAP 6: Capture of Tololing

two localities and around Tololing, including at Point 4590. They had constructed bunkers along the ridgeline and were well stocked with ration and ammunition.

The lessons learnt from the previous attacks on Tololing were applied and a different type of plan was approved by Major General Mohinder Puri, General Officer Commanding, 8 Mountain Division. He had recently taken charge of the battles here. A multidirectional plan of attack was formulated, in which several battalions were to take part simultaneously. This would surprise the enemy, and keep him guessing as to where the attack was building up, as well as divide his reactions.

Sufficient artillery support was vital to this plan, but it was difficult to allot adequate artillery fire units to each assaulting battalion if all of them started their attack at the same time. However, multidirectional attacks must start the attack at the same time; otherwise the enemy would guess and take appropriate action. A solution was needed and therefore, a decision was taken to have a staggered 'H' hour*; meaning attacks will commence simultaneously within half an hour to forty-five minutes of each other, to give adequate fire support to each assaulting column, before shifting to another to not compromise the essence of the multidirectional attack strategy. The overall plan of attack was:

- 2 RAJ RIF was to capture Tololing by 0600 hours on 13$^{th}$ June.
- 18 GARH RIF (18$^{th}$ Battalion of the Garhwal Rifles Regiment) was to capture Point 5140 by 0700 hours on 13$^{th}$ June.
- 18 GREN was to provide the firm base for the attack on Tololing as they were in contact with the enemy and knew their exact location. On the request of 2 RAJ RIF, they were to provide a clean passage for the assaulting troops by withdrawing 150 metres from the Barbad Bunker, captured partially in the last battle. It was an emotional moment for them as a lot of blood had been sacrificed on it; but they agreed.

~

For Lt Col M.B. Ravindra Nath, the CO 2 RAJ RIF, many details had to be ironed out to finalize his plan. The exact strength of the intruders and their location on the top were still unknown. To ascertain these, each Company Commander was asked to carry out reconnaissance personally. Each one of them was asked to give their plan of attack on Tololing.

The balance battalion utilized the time to carry ammunition as close to the front as possible. At such heights, it is difficult to carry one's own weight and, with an additional 20–30 kgs of

---

* H Hour is the exact time the attack begins and all other timings are related to it. For example, H+30 would mean 30 minutes after H hour.

ammunition, it was an arduous task to make the treacherous climb! The ammunition itself needed 850 men to carry it up. Tradesmen, such as barbers, safai-walas, washermen and clerks, who generally remain at the bases, were so charged up that they volunteered to go up with the loads. One such washerman had night blindness, but refused to stay back! He caught the 'coat-tails' of the soldier in front, and delivered his load. The next two nights were utilized to lug up the ration.

Our artillery by now had built up. A massive barrage of fire started a few days prior to the attack to allow Pakistani intruders no time to relax on Tololing. The aim was to be able to cause as much destruction on the Tololing defences as possible. The intruders had no permanent bunkers there, but the moment the artillery fire would start, they would go back and down the hill, till the fire was lifted. Thus, only marginal damage was done to them. They had cut rocks and had gone into them like foxes into foxholes. Their preparation of defences seemed to be a few months old at some places.

The Company Commanders had finished their reconnaissance and had reported that only up to two platoons could move upwards on the southeast spur and reach an area called Ledge safely. In the southwest direction, Patthar was the only safe point to reach, but only one platoon at a time could go ahead beyond it. There was no other way one could climb up and attack Tololing. Plans were further refined and preparations went into full swing.

Although the temperatures had dipped below zero degrees at night prior to the attack on 12$^{th}$ June 1999, the boys geared themselves up in their combat fatigues, coats, boots and steel helmets. No one was to carry anything but a pouch full of ammunition, one packed meal and one bottle of water.

The troops that were to go for the first attack had been given two nights to rest. A night prior to the attack, they had moved up as far forward as possible. Even though artillery shells were pounding all over, some rest was taken. Prayers were offered; the Battalion Panditji tied rakhis (the symbolic thread of protection) to the CO and all Company Commanders. He put tilak on the forehead of all the soldiers as a blessing from the gods. Letters home were hurriedly written; some of them were to be the last.... Nobody knows for whom the bell tolls, but each one knew he could lay his life down.

'Tololing has to be captured!' were the last orders of the CO, before the march began.

The enthusiastic response was, 'Please come and have breakfast in the morning with us, Sir! Raja Ram Chandra ki jai.'

From a distance, Tololing looks like a single feature, but a closer look revealed that it could be divided into Tololing Top, with a flat area nearby and Point 4590 with Barbad Bunker, Rock and South Spur around it (See map 6).

The battalion plan indicated that Major Vivek Gupta would lead the assault from the southeast, and head for Tololing Top and the flat area directly, with his two platoons leading. To the southwest, only one platoon could go ahead to capture Point 4590, Rock and Barbad Bunker.

A quick staff check revealed that while our own artillery could provide support for attack on Tololing Top and the flat area, Barbad Bunker on the southwest could not be reached by our Artillery. Since it was the only workable plan, this handicap was accepted. To deceive the enemy, it was decided that the attack should first be launched on Point 4590, so that the enemy vacates Tololing Top to hold the point. A meticulous fire plan was also worked out for the artillery, to deceive the enemy and not give away our intentions.

A platoon of Delta Company started for the first assault on Rock and Point 4590 at 2100 hours on 12$^{th}$ June. It took two hours before this team, under Major Mohit Saxena, could close onto area Rock. With a bit of luck on their side, a lodgement on area Rock was soon established without encountering much opposition. Rock was made the base for the attack on Point 4590 as it was barely thirty metres away. How to get past the wall of bullets, however?

While Delta Company prepared itself to attack Point 4590 from area Rock, Charlie Company under Major Gupta, half an hour later, also found their way to the Flat Area without giving the enemy any inkling about their movement. The enemy, in fact, had fallen prey to the attack strategy and had practically vacated Flat Area to strengthen Point 4590 where they thought the attack was heading.

Subedar Dharambir, the platoon leader, occupied Flat Area but as his radio set was damaged, he couldn't pass on the good news to his Company Commander. Lt Parveen Tomar, meanwhile, took control of his platoon and rushed towards Tololing Top at midnight. By then, the enemy had realized his folly and started to recall men from Point 4590, where Major Mohit Saxena was giving them a tough fight in his quest to capture it.

As a result of the shrewd plan, the enemy faced a dilemma: whether to launch a counter-attack at Point 4590 or to reinforce Tololing Top. They probably chose to counter-attack at Point 4590 first, which they had already lost. They succeeded in pushing back the handful of our men who had occupied Point 4590, and then they sent some troops to reinforce Tololing Top.

Subedar Karam Singh fell back to Rock from Point 4590. The enemy was now getting ready to counter-attack at Rock. These men continued to hold on to their small lodgment at Rock amidst a barrage of fire as the enemy made numerous desperate attempts to recapture it.

Meanwhile, the battle on Tololing Top was reaching its zenith, with Lt Tomar advancing inch by inch, taking cover behind boulders. A MMG situated there blurted out molten metal with unimaginable ferocity, taking the lives of two of our brave JCOs.

The CO now ordered Major Gupta to open a new front and attack Tololing Top from further right of Lt Tomar. While this outflanking manoeuvre was being undertaken, Subedar Dharambir started to fire at the enemy at Barbad Bunker from the Flat Area behind it. Major Vivek Gupta, in turn, told his platoon to go through Flat Area, which they did, to reach five metres short of the Tololing Top. The enemy was taken by surprise; and a heavy battle at close quarters ensued.

Manning a light machine gun (LMG) and leading his depleted section,* Naik Shri Bhagwan charged at the enemy occupying the Tololing Top. The enemy was forced to withdraw from the Top. They ran down to the other side towards a sangar† twenty metres away. Meanwhile, Major Mohit Saxena was still battling to recapture Point 4590. After a heavy exchange of fire, he, too, succeeded.

Major Vivek Gupta immediately rushed his entire platoon to the Top and held onto the position. His radio operator had not been able to join him yet, so he couldn't pass this news to the CO.

The enemy now collected its men by pulling out troops from other locations and started launching counter-attacks on Tololing Top from this sangar. Meanwhile, the CO decided to climb up to Tololing Top himself. A firefight was on: the enemy would rush towards the top and our soldiers would get up and shoot at them. Around an hour past midnight, a bullet found its way to Major Vivek Gupta, killing him on the spot in Area Flat on the Top.

Major Gupta had had a reputation of not resting until the task assigned to him was completed; now, he could rest in peace, forever. The battalion remembers him as a good singer. He was a keen bodybuilder, too, and had been declared Mr Gwalior just before the battalion had moved to the valley. Far away at Mhow, Captain Raj Shree Gupta, his wife, who was posted there as

---
* A section is the smallest sub-unit of a battalion and consists of ten soldiers. A platoon consists of three such sections.

† A bunker constructed of the available rocks, without cement

an army doctor, woke up after a bad dream sweating all over. Someone was making his final journey to the heavens. A cool breeze touched her, and went past, never to return again.

The CO reached the Tololing Top at three o'clock and found the dead bodies of his men strewn all over. Tears welled up in his eyes, as he ordered his Second-in-Command, Major Bajaj, to ensure that Barbad Bunker was captured.

When Major Bajaj reached the Barbad Bunker area, he found Major Adhikari's body, which had been lying there since 30th May. He sent Havildar Durga with a few men to recover it, but Durga and two others got injured when an explosive tied to the leg of the officer went off. The Pakistanis had booby-trapped the body!

The frenzy of battle was at its peak when Major Bajaj was witness to a gory sight, that of a soldier slaughtering an enemy, slowly, with his bayonet. This furious man was the 'sahayak', a constant companion of Major Gupta, and before he could be stopped, he had finished this act; basically to avenge the killing of his 'sahib'.

Barbad Bunker was captured at the break of dawn, and with the end of the macabre night, all of Tololing was taken.

The radio message that reached Brigadier Amar Aul at dawn, said, 'Tololing is with us!' He received the news with mixed emotions; tremendous joy, pride and sorrow. While the nation rose in ovation to the first victory, a rain of artillery shells from the enemy started pounding Tololing, even before the first rays of the sun could bathe the gallants.

The devastating effect of artillery shelling was visible all around. The color of Tololing had changed, from muddy brown to a burnt-out reddish hue. Artillery guns had fired almost twenty thousand bombs. If that many bombs were to fall on a township, they would flatten the entire area into rubble. The Bofors guns did a lot of good; a direct shot gave ample cover and enabled our infantry men to close in on the enemy.

After the shelling Lt Col M.B. Ravindra Nath, the CO of the

battalion, saw a large number of his soldiers lying dead in front of him. Twenty-five men were wounded and some of them were in critical condition, in need of immediate medical assistance. And that was going to be a challenge. Each injured man needed the shoulders of almost eight to take him down to the nearest road head, taking eight to ten hours on the way. Helicopters could not reach them up on the Top due to heavy enemy presence. Amidst the artillery fire, the caravan of injured men trickled down the hill.

The CO was also worried that the battalion's ammunition was almost exhausted and another counter-attack by the enemy would be fatal. Immediate replenishment was vital. Certain readjustments were carried out to ensure that essential weapons could beat back a desperate attempt by the enemy. But the sight of the dead enemy soldiers lying around convinced him that any further counter-attack by them was unlikely. Identity Cards on the dead men showed that they belonged to 6 Northern Light Infantry of Pakistan Regular Army, and that they were *not* militants, as had been claimed. Gas masks were also recovered, suggesting that Pakistan had used chemical weapons against Indian soldiers. Nausea, choking and a burning sensation in the eyes had been earlier felt by Major Vivek Gupta's company, evidently as a result of the use of chemical weapons; their bodies had typical chemical burn marks on their backs.

Finally, the enemy shelling on Tololing halted for some time. Telephone lines were reconnected by the signallers of the battalion. The operator passed on the handset to the CO; the Chief of the Army Staff (COAS) was coming on the line to compliment him, as his battalion had done the nation a great service that would go down in history. The infectious courage and willpower of these heroes were being passed onto the entire nation. An Indian Tsunami had come, and the recapture of Tololing was turning the tide of the war.

Several acts of bravery by 2 RAJ RIF, in the battle on Tololing and subsequently in other battles, were recognized. Three Maha Vir Chakras, including one to Major Vivek Gupta, four Vir Chakras, including one to the CO, and four Sena Medals were awarded to the battalion. More of these awards were yet to come. Their tales of legendary bravery continue to echo in the history of Indian Army, and will inspire the coming generations of our great nation.

# Cavemen at Point 5140

While Tololing was being tackled, a simultaneous assault on Point 5140 was planned to ease pressure on Tololing, and this task was given to Colonel S.K. Chakravarti (Chaks), the CO of 18 Garhwal Rifles (18 GARH RIF); an infantry battalion that had recently arrived in the battlefield and relieved the companies of 1 NAGA in contact with the enemy, on 4$^{th}$ and 5$^{th}$ June.

The plan was drawn off the map as extensive reconnaissance was not easy without detection, and the enemy was very sensitive to any movement from the side of Bimbat Nala through which 1 NAGA had earlier attempted their attack. They had noticed enhanced activities taking place in Bimbat Nala despite 18 GARH RIF confining its movements to the night, and kept firing machine guns and artillery at the Administrative Base. Heavy firing on the day of the attack was to commence on 12$^{th}$ June.

The advance upwards was very slow. The enemy was constantly interfering and making it extremely difficult for the Garhwalis to progress. A combination of treacherous terrain, with huge rocks and gaps filled with hardened snow, and heavy firing from the enemy delayed them inordinately on their way to the mountaintop. One of the companies was less than a hundred metres short of the ridgeline. The moon was still hanging low in the sky and the enemy bunkers were in sight, but daylight was not far away—to press home the attack would mean heavy losses to our own troops. No reserves were readily available behind them. They had to rush back to the firm base.

However, a section worth of men under the leadership of two JCOs were caught under enemy fire and were not traceable throughout the day. Lt Sumeet Roy took a patrol out, voluntarily, and was able to bring them back down by midnight.[*]

Another Company of 18 GARH RIF had reached their objective on the ridgeline as well, before dawn. As they were preparing to advance, they found themselves trapped from three sides by the enemy. Heavy firing caught them in the open and Pakistani machine guns and rockets injured nine of their men. Some of them managed to hurriedly huddle up in a small cave, while the others managed to return to the base. Colonel Chakravarty ordered all his men back to the firm base.

The men later recounted that they felt a divine presence in the icy cave of the Himalayas. Perhaps the souls of the rishi-munis of yore blessed them and so they survived. Who knows?

---

[*] Bammi, Lt Gen Y.M., (Retd), *Kargil*, pp. 221–22.

# Huffs and Humps

Once Tololing was captured by 2 RAJ RIF, they moved two companies up there and were further placed as reserves to 18 GREN who were poised to use Tololing as a firm base. By doing so, they could capture a series of Humps on the ridgeline which led to Point 5140 in the north (See Map 7). Since the attack on Point 5140 by 18 GARH RIF could not progress as planned, the battalion was to launch another attack on it on the night of 13th June, in conjunction with 18 GREN heading for the Humps.

While these operations were being launched, Prime Minister Atal Bihari Vajpayee was scheduled to visit the HQ of 8 Mountain Division on 13th June, but he got delayed by a few hours as he had proceeded to address the troops in Kargil, instead. However, since one of the batteries* of Bofors, which had supported the attack on Tololing just the previous evening from the same location was near the Division HQ in Matayin, the Pakistanis had started pounding the area heavily with their artillery shells from across the LOC. The troops, who had begun congregating there for the prime minister's visit, ran to take shelter. The helicopter, parked nearby, also took off immediately. The intensity of shelling increased, but fortunately there were no immediate human casualties. Shelling continued for two hours, destroying everything with its impact. The Division HQ had to be relocated immediately in Mughalpura for the rest of

---

* A battery is a sub-unit of an artillery regiment.

the period, but not before a senior Signals Officer was badly wounded. The prime minister's visit to the Division HQ was cancelled due to these circumstances.[*]

The loss of Tololing had made the Pakistanis furious and they put forth all their might to regain it. As the day of 13th June started fading, the Alpha and Charlie Company of 18 GREN were near the staging area on Tololing. A sudden burst of enemy artillery fire thwarted their progress towards Hump. Eleven fatal and seventeen injured casualties, in a matter of minutes! The enemy had started shelling heavily in retaliation.

It was a very unfortunate thing to have happened when the move was just beginning. Almost a platoon worth of troops got pushed off the battle scene. They needed a breather to reorganize themselves. But to wait there would have become too costly for subsequent battles, as the enemy was quickly reinforcing the areas on the way of the Indian Tsunami heading towards the LOC. Therefore, the H hour was delayed by only two hours, just long enough to enable them to send the injured back down.

The angry Grenadiers were now doubly resolved. They started their operations and, by morning, had captured a part of Hump. By mid-day they had secured their share of the seven Humps.

---

[*] Puri, Lt. Gen. Mohinder, PVSM, UYSM, *Kargil: Turning the Tide* (New Delhi: Lancer Publishers, 2015), p. 68.

# Rocky Knob

In the meanwhile, 13 Jammu & Kashmir Rifles (13 JAK RIF) in the Kashmir Valley, was ordered to move in for the operations. They had concentrated at Gumri within two days and had started acclimatization. On their fourth day there, they were told to wait as reserves for the attack on Tololing by 2 RAJ RIF, described in 'Turning the Tide in Dras'.

On the morning of $14^{th}$ June, two companies of 13 JAK RIF climbed up and reached the freshly captured Tololing Top, under Lt Col Yogesh Joshi who had just been promoted from the rank of Major, in situ. He had just put on the shoulder badges sent by Maj Gen Mohinder Puri, the General Officer commanding the 8 Mountain Division, who had taken charge as the Officiating CO of 13 JAK RIF. The CO had been evacuated due to high altitude sickness.

They identified the objectives and prepared for an assault on Rocky Knob later in the night.

It was the night of $15^{th}$ June. The attack by 13 JAK RIF began with Alpha Company in the lead and Charlie Company right behind. They occupied a feature called Hump Eight. Heavy enemy fire rained down on them from a feature that had been hidden earlier. Two Humps, Nine and Ten were still occupied by the enemy. Two of our soldiers were hit by enemy sniper fire and a third one got a burst of universal machine gun (UMG) fire on his face.

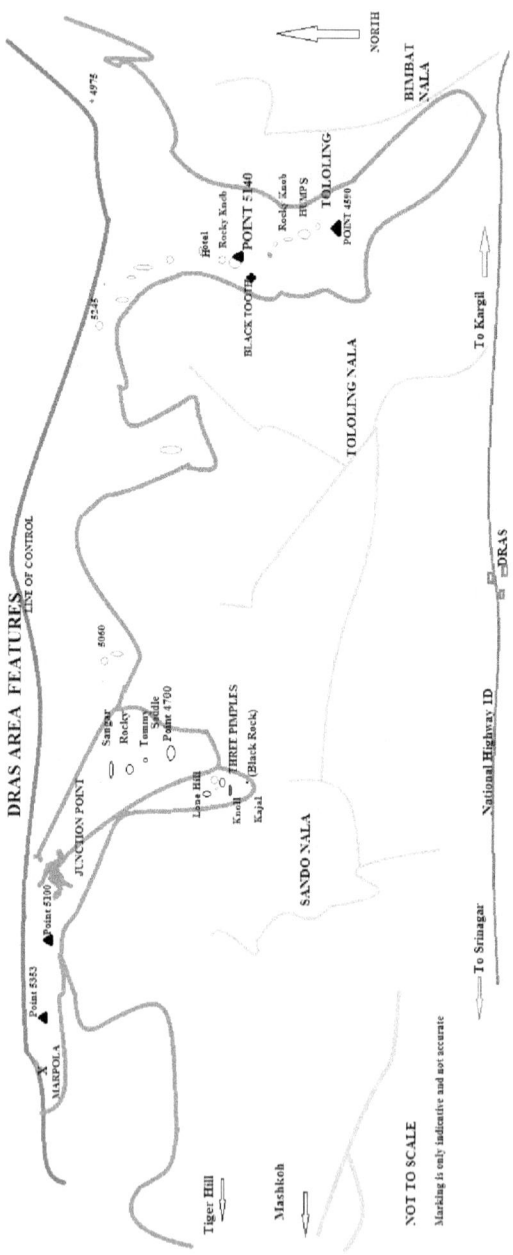

MAP 7: Dras Area Features

A heavy firefight ensued. The leading company's MMG ran short of ammunition. There was a dire need to have some sort of supporting fire to progress the attack. Before the ammunition could be fetched up, the only alternative available was to ask for an artillery SOS fire which was used—a dangerous last resort to bring down fire from our own batteries onto the location, and thus hold the enemy at bay. The calls over the radio for SOS fire remained unanswered. There was no alternative but to wait till the ammunition for the MMG could arrive.

When they came, the MMG ammunition and missiles brought hope, but the enemy was well entrenched and in a position of advantage. Would they be able to succeed? Dawn was ready to break; there was no choice but to wait for the sun to set again.

## Thumbs Up to Point 5140

On the night of 17$^{th}$ June, Bofors, located at Dras, took a direct shot at a bunker on Hump Nine. The attack had begun and Alpha Company was successful in capturing Hump Nine, Hump Ten and Rocky Knob! Another small feature, popularly known as 'Thumbs Up', was also captured by 13 JAK RIF. The enemy fled, leaving behind two of its dead. One of these was Naik Noor Mohammed of 6 Northern Light Infantry (6NLI) of the Pakistan Army. The UMGs left behind by them were, ironically, turned around and fired at them while they were fleeing!

The Regimental Medical Officer (RMO) present at the Top deserves a prominent place in history. It was time for Captain (Dr) Ajay, just out of Amravati Medical College, to live out the oath he had made towards his profession. He had been called up to Rocky Knob from Hump III to treat the injured soldiers. Although it was only a few hundred metres away, it would take him about twenty minutes to reach Rocky Knob. He was advised to keep away from the track as it was in direct view and fire of the enemy. But how else would he be able to reach his patients in time? Ajay wasted no time and started running along the track. He was seen, and greeted with a burst of fire. He ran as fast as his legs would take him and the bullets initially chased him close on his heels. The hands of my Saviour are bigger than those of the killers; I am on a mission to save lives and will surely make it, he thought. He was now chasing the bullets which were directed ahead of him. It was the longest ever run for him and for everyone watching. Seven minutes is all he took to reach Rocky Knob! He was welcomed with a good-humoured jibe that he could bring home an Olympic gold medal.

Captain Ajay did not waste time and started attending to the wounded, lying all around him. At this point, the enemy started firing artillery shells on Rocky Knob! While he stitched up a wounded soldier, a shell landed near him, directly onto the dead body of the Pakistani soldier, Noor Mohammed, and blew off its hand.

While this operation was in progress, the enemy continued firing their artillery at the 13 JAK RIF base in Bimbat Nala. Major Jasrotia, the son of DIG BSF, Jammu, was caught in the open and hit by shrapnel in the back. Almost ten others were also injured in the shelling. The officer, despite bleeding profusely, ran to evacuate those injured. Major Rajiv told him to be evacuated himself, but he refused until he had evacuated all the others. While doing so, he collapsed and was forcefully evacuated to the ADS (Advance Dressing Station). Unfortunately, due to the loss of blood, he died en route. By then, twenty of the soldiers were wounded, and four had attained martyrdom.

# Call Sign of Colas

While the Rocky Knob was being captured, the two other Company Commanders, Captain Sanjiv Singh Jamwal, Bravo Company and Captain Vikram Batra, Delta Company were busy carrying out reconnaissance of the routes to Point 5140.

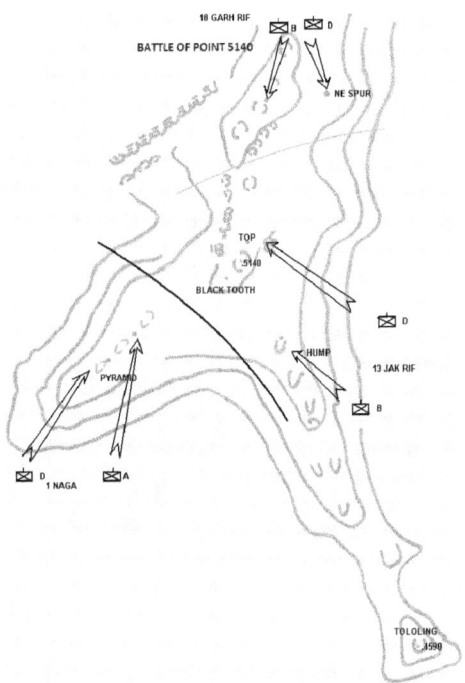

MAP 8: Capture of Point 5140

The final multidirectional attack plan was to press home the attack by 13 JAK RIF, using two companies from the south and southeast directions, by establishing a fire base* at Rocky Knob. The Naga Battalion was to assault from the further left and, once again, 18 GARH RIF was tasked to come up from the northeast.

~

Captain S.S. Jamwal and Captain Vikram Batra were waiting to see the devastation caused by the Bofors guns, firing direct onto the Point 5140 enemy bunkers. By 2030 hours on 19th June, the direct hits by Bofors onto the enemy were pushing them inside their bunkers. These two companies began their movement towards the objective, Point 5140, 500–600 metres upwards, but they were expected to take about three hours to reach there.

Our artillery was giving fire support and was firing very close to the advancing troops. Six hours, and the troops had come within 20 metres of the enemy. As their movement was comparatively silent, the enemy assumed that the attack was building up from the west and northeast, where there was a lot of exchange of fire. The Bravo Company reached the first sangar and the enemy was taken by complete surprise; exchange of fire left three of the enemy dead.

Pakistani JCO, Subedar Saeed Ahmed Shah, in charge of those Seven Bunkers on the top, came up on the radio net and called up Captain Vikram Batra. He abused him in Punjabi and then threatened him in chaste Urdu, saying 'Shershah aa to gaye, wapis nahin ja paoge!' A further exchange of abuses followed on the radio set. Sangar to sangar, both the companies fought the enemy and killed many, including the Pakistani JCO. His personal diary revealed his identification. He was from Pak Regular Army,

---

*The heavy automatic firing weapons and missiles are collectively placed at one spot, to facilitate the last 100-metre advance of the assaulting troops, since the artillery stops firing at this range for fear of causing injury to own troops

6 Northern Light Battalion. His last wish, recorded in his diary said, 'I should be buried in my birthplace, Banihal (Kashmir Valley), instead of in Pakistan.' However, international military norms do not permit this and his body was later handed over to Pakistan.

The remaining enemy soldiers ran away, leaving behind a large number of weapons, equipment and rations, all inside a fibreglass cookhouse on the top. Freshly cooked halwa was found in their frying pan!

It was time for Captain Vikram Batra to give the success signal to his CO. He crackled on his radio set: 'Yeh dil maange more!'

# Magic at Black Tooth

While 13 JAK RIF was busy capturing Point 5140, 1 NAGA had been tasked to capture another Rocky Knob and a feature called Black Tooth in the close vicinity of Point 5140 (See Map 8). Their plan was to capture Rocky Knob with Alpha Company under Captain Y.S. Gill, and Black Tooth and Pimple with Bravo Company under Major Madan.

By 18$^{th}$ June, the battalion had moved to their firm bases in Tololing Nala. The attack on Rocky Knob succeeded as planned on the night of 19$^{th}$ June. However, Bravo Company confronted a near vertical 60-foot-high cliff, and their attempts to scale the height did not succeed the whole night. As the company was in danger of being spotted at day-break, the CO ordered them to join Alpha Company at Rocky Knob.

To negotiate the vertical cliff, specialist mountaineering equipment and trained mountaineers were required to lead the assault. The expert team of HAWS (High Altitude Warfare School) was requisitioned and they arrived on the third day, i.e. 23$^{rd}$ June. Meanwhile, the troops were being subjected to artillery shelling. On the night of the 23$^{rd}$, a fresh attempt to capture Black Tooth was made. The expert team fixed ropes so that the troops following behind could climb up. It was still almost three to four hours of difficult going and by midnight, the company had reached the top of the Black Tooth area.

They found that there were two Pimples separated by a small cliff. Both of them were occupied by the enemy who had laid two ladders so that they could freely move from one to the other. When our troops reached the top, the enemy quietly removed one of the ladders. There was no way for our troops to jump across to the other side. To them, it appeared that a piece of land was magically removed! How did the Pakistanis go from there? Did they use some kind of talisman in this voodoo land?[*] Only when our troops recovered the ladder later, did they get an answer to these intriguing questions.

Furthermore, the Pakistanis started pounding them with artillery shells and automatic fire, and placed booby traps in the target area so that no move across to Pimple II was possible. They, thus, made the area unassailable.

Unabashedly, the Naga troops continued to put pressure to capture the rest of the target. By now, Point 5140 had fallen and the enemy had started fleeing as they felt that they were being encircled from three directions. Once they noticed that one of our platoons had gone behind them to cut them off, they abandoned their positions and ran towards the LOC. The Naga troops seized the opportunity and captured the entire Black Tooth area by the first light on 24th June.

A great deal of ammunition and rations were left behind by the fleeing enemy. Pakistan Army Canteen bills of 6 NLI were recovered, proving yet again, the identity of the enemy on Black Tooth. In this entire operation, other than minor injuries, there was no casualty to our troops.

By 28th June, 13 J&K RIF and 2 RAJ RIF were told to withdraw for further operations and the entire area was occupied by 1 NAGA. 18 GARH RIF was also pulled back and assigned another objective, Point 4700. 1 NAGA was asked to send troops to occupy Swami I and Swami II posts on the east of Bimbat Nala, towards the LOC.

---

[*] Soldiers have many such wartime stories which are not true, but are often circulated and believed in widely, even after the war. This belief was not true, but it is mentioned only to highlight the mindset during a war.

# Proud of Three Pimples

Tololing and Point 5140 had been cleared of the enemy. To maintain the momentum, the focus had shifted to Point 5060, which was at a dominating height just close to the LOC (See Map 7).

2 RAJ RIF was tasked with carrying out reconnaissance on 20th June. The reconnaissance parties found that the troops had to first get past Point 4700 to reach Point 5060. Therefore, it was important that it be cleared first—which meant launching another attack.

Further reconnaissance confirmed that an area called Three Pimples Ridge would have to be captured in conjunction with Point 4700 in the first phase by one battalion each. In subsequent phases, it would be better to capture Point 5100 rather than Point 5060 to reach the LOC faster—the ultimate goal of all these attacks.

The Three Pimple Ridge, which emanated from Point 5100 on the Marpo La Ridgeline, was to the west of Tololing Nala. It bifurcated into two ridgelines at Junction Point, one ridge going towards Point 4700 and the other ridge moving south towards Lone Hill and Three Pimples. Thus, any attempt to capture Point 4700 would have been interfered with by the enemy's presence at Three Pimples. Besides this, Three Pimples effectively dominated the National Highway, the Dras town and Sando valley.

Capture of this area would pave the way for capturing Point

5100 and subsequently Point 5060, thus effectively isolating all intrusion east of Sando Nala in Dras. Three Pimples, alias Black Rock complex, itself consisted of Three Pimples, Lone Hill, Knoll and Kajal and bifurcated into two spur lines along the southeast and southwest. Point 4700 Ridge consisted of Point 4700, Saddle, Tommy, Rocky, Sangar and Junction Point, which were a series of objectives to be recaptured from the enemy (See Map 9).

The enemy had had the maximum amount of time to prepare a network of defences here, and had a well-coordinated set-up supported by effective artillery. A bold plan to launch multidirectional attacks and capture maximum localities was chalked out.

In the first phase of the attack, 2 RAJ RIF was to capture Knoll and Lone Hill and contact Junction Point by early morning on 29th June.

18 GARH RIF was asked to capture Tommy, Saddle and Point 4700 by the same time.

In the second phase of the attack, 2 RAJ RIF was required to clear Three Pimples by midday and 16 GRENADIERS (16 GREN) were to exploit the situation along the southwest ridge and capture Junction Point by 30th June.

18 GARH RIF had been tasked with capturing Rocky and Sangar and were to link up with 16 GREN at Junction Point by the morning of 30th June.

By 25th June, 2 RAJ RIF had been building up ahead close to the base of Three Pimples and they needed another two to three nights to build their administrative load before finally launching the attack. Registration of targets had begun on both the sides. The enemy had, somehow, sensed that the attack was building up. That is why their artillery was continuously landing in the close vicinity of the assembling troops. But by now, our troops had learnt their lessons and had sited themselves so well that the enemy could not reach them.

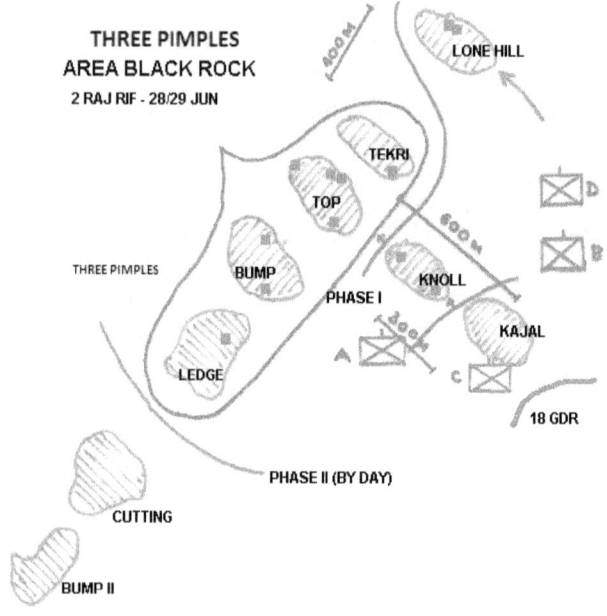

MAP 9: Capture of Three Pimples/Area Black Rock

The attack by 2 RAJ RIF and 18 GARH RIF had been staggered, so that 2 RAJ RIF were to begin, while 18 GARH RIF were to attack two hours later at midnight. Such an arrangement also facilitated each of them getting adequate artillery support, so that each attack was provided fire units as required.

~

The attack by 2 RAJ RIF was to be launched on the night of 28th June, with Alpha Company, under Major Padmapani Acharya, to head for the Knoll. Their firm base was to be established only 600–700 metres short of the Knoll. A name was required for this location, but nothing seemed to fit. Just then, the CO asked Major Acharya to suggest a name, and that is how this spot was named Kajal!

Delta Company under Major Mohit Saxena was tasked with

capturing Lone Hill, while Bravo Company was to rush towards the Junction area after the fall of Lone Hill.

Before the attack, Major Mohit Saxena was sent on the night of 27$^{th}$ June to carry out further reconnaissance towards Lone Hill. On his return, he gave the disturbing news that there were still two more small enemy outposts before Lone Hill. It was important to prevent any interference from these features, and the only way to do that was to take a circuitous route north of Lone Hill, before assaulting it.

The Ghatak platoon[*] was under the command of Captain Neikezhakuo Kenguruse. He was extremely fit and could outrun the other commandos with a heavy rocket launcher on his back. Hailing from Kohima in Nagaland, he was engaged to a doctor back home. Captain Kenguruse was very popular with his troops and was affectionately known as Naga Saheb or Nimbu Saheb amongst them. A good guitarist, singer and drummer, he was deeply religious as well. I had known him while his battalion was undergoing pre-induction training at Kashmir. I had to tick him off one day, because while playing basketball, he wouldn't pass the ball to anyone. But he scored every time he took the ball back thereafter! He was to score big yet again, when he was specially chosen and sent ahead to prevent any enemy movement to and from the Three Pimple area.

~

The attack began at 2030 hours on 28$^{th}$ June. As Lt Vijyant Thapar, a young officer from NOIDA, was concentrating his platoon to launch the attack, enemy artillery was finally able to catch up with him. It killed two of his men and injured seven others. The platoon was ordered to recoup itself and placed in reserve. Major Acharya now led the assaulting troops.

---

[*] His daughter, Aparajita Acharya, recently penned a tribute to her father in *Our Babloo: The Hero of Drass*..

Knoll had two enemy sangars. The first was soon captured. However, the next one was still firing and holding on. Acharya called one of his JCOs aside and started working out a plan to tackle this position. It was around midnight when the enemy saw them closing in. A hand grenade landed between Major Acharya and the JCO. Major P. Acharya lost his life in the explosion, while the JCO was severely wounded in the thigh.

Major Acharya had been very close to his men and was loved by them as he could speak to them in their own language, despite not being from the area. He was always the Master of Ceremonies at the functions held in the battalion. He had been married just a few months ago.* The sad news about Major Acharya's death was conveyed to the CO, who was shocked to lose him, but maintained his poise and urged the company to not lose courage, and instead to continue striving to achieve their goal.

Lt Vijyant Thapar had by now regained his command and control. He was ordered to take control of the situation at the Knoll. On reaching the scene of battle, Lt Thapar quickly assessed that while this sangar was holding onto the Knoll, the enemy could not be defeated. He ordered his men to follow him while he personally assaulted the enemy sangar. He wanted to avenge the killing of Major Acharya. Lt Vijyant Thapar was barely a few feet away from the enemy sangar when a burst of fire tore through him, killing him instantly.

Vijyant was a fourth-generation military officer; his father is a retired colonel. He was fond of cricket and music. He had shared an audio cassette full of peppy songs with me while under training at the Corps Battle School just before this war. He left behind an emotional note to his parents. One of his obituaries read, 'A soldier at 19, an officer at 20 and a martyr at 22.'

---

*His daughter, Aparajita Acharya, recently penned a tribute to her father in *Our Babloo: The Hero of Drass*.

With the Company Commander and second-in-command having lost their lives, the responsibility for capturing the objective fell upon the shoulders of a brave Subedar, Shivraj Singh. The CO was informed that ammunition was running out and that Shivraj had only a few men to continue the battle. Naib Subedar Bhopinder was ordered to carry ammunition and reinforce the beleaguered Subedar Shivraj Singh and his men.

In the confusion and chaos of the battlefront, Bhopinder was, unfortunately, unable to link up with Shivraj Singh. Instead, Major Bajaj, who was heading towards Junction Point with Bravo Company, was redirected to link up with Shivraj at Knoll. However, he, too, could not do so.

As time was running out, Shivraj Singh requested the CO to take direct artillery shoots onto this sangar. As this was dangerous, the troops had to go into hiding close by for a few minutes when the shots were being taken. The direct hit was an instant success and the sangar fell silent. Shivraj and his men finally charged at it to mop up the remnants. Major Bajaj and Bhopinder could only join them by early dawn. The Knoll had been captured, but not before the sacrifices of so many of our brave men.

~

Delta Company, under Major Mohit Saxena, headed for Lone Hill. However, after some time, he went out of radio communication. A fresh radio set was dispatched. Only after it reached Major Saxena, did the CO come to know that heavy fighting at Lone Hill had resulted in a lot of casualties and that the attack had stalled.

Major Saxena informed the CO that Captain Kenguruse's party had attempted to climb Lone Hill from the direction of the almost vertical cliff, and had managed to almost reach the top, barefooted, in the slippery snowbound area. However, the complete party had been shot down, and he had fallen 200 feet off the cliff. There were other casualties too but the actual situation could not be ascertained at night.

The CO asked the Brigade Commander if he could withdraw this company which was in an inferior position, with no cover available. The Brigade Commander initially asked him to hold on but as daylight was about to break in another two hours, he agreed to pull them back.

On seeing the Indian troops returning from Lone Hill, the enemy felt cut off from his rear and, fearing attack from three sides, started withdrawing from Three Pimples. Major Mohit Saxena's company caught them out in the open. In the ensuing firefight, the enemy suffered heavy casualties and started fleeing. Major Saxena reached the Firm Base, Kajal. All the injured were evacuated and Major Saxena prepared to return with a fresh platoon from Bravo Company.

In the meantime, Major Bajaj moved towards a feature called Tekri on Three Pimples from Knoll. He found it unoccupied, and our troops occupied the sangars immediately. Suddenly, the enemy started firing from close by, and two of our soldiers died. However, there was no counter-attack.

On his return to Lone Hill, Major Saxena realized that the enemy was withdrawing from Lone Hill too; the guns on the other side had suddenly fallen silent. Could it be a ruse by the enemy? It was now time to capture Lone Hill, or occupy it while it stood empty! A daylight attempt was made. The attack succeeded and Lone Hill was in the hands of our troops.

The battle had taken a very heavy toll on our men. In the entire operation, three officers and ten men from other ranks[*] had sacrificed their lives. Fifty-one men from other ranks were injured, out of which thirty-six were critical. However, plenty of arms and ammunition were recovered, including five machine guns. The Company Commander's documents, including maps

---

[*] Soldiers of all ranks below JCO.

marked with Pakistani artillery positions were also captured, alongside his personal clothing and equipment. The sangars of the enemy were very strong and had not been affected by our artillery firing; only one of them was found to be slightly damaged. This suggested that the enemy had had a lot of time at hand to prepare these sangars, and strengthen them.

It appeared that the Three Pimple area had been strongly held by a single company, with their route of maintenance along the nalas—as opposed to along the ridgelines, as commonly believed earlier. This reality emerged during the day. Major Mohit Saxena recounted cutting telephone cables along the nala during the night, but at that time, it did not strike anybody that it could well be their route of maintenance.

The battalion started coming down on 3rd July and concentrated in Dras by 5th July, for a well-deserved rest and refit.

Major Acharya and Captain Kenguruse were awarded Maha Vir Chakras posthumously, while Major Saxena and Lt Thapar (posthumous) were honoured with Vir Chakras.[*]

---

[*] Not all awards have been listed here; please see the official lists for the full list of awards.

# Complex Captured (Point 4700)

While Three Pimples was being captured by 2 RAJ RIF, 18 GARH RIF was continuing their operations towards the Point 4700 Complex, which included Tommy, Saddle and Point 4700. They were tasked with capturing this by 0600 hours on 29th June. In the subsequent phase, 16 GREN was to deploy along the southwestern ridgeline and capture a feature called Junction Point, by the next morning. 18 GARH RIF was to establish a link up with 16 GREN at Junction Point at the same time, after having captured Rocky and Sangar. As the artillery guns were required to fire and assist 2 RAJ RIF in the capture of Three Pimples and, also, 18 GARH RIF for the Point 4700 Complex, the fire plan was staggered to meet both the requirements.

The operations commenced as per plan, and Charlie and Delta Companies left the firm base at 2030 hours and 2050 hours, respectively. The move from the base to the objectives was treacherous, with the enemy continuously engaging the advancing troops with artillery and automatic weapons.

The enemy was well entrenched at Tommy and Point 4700, and fierce hand-to-hand fighting took place for the capture of sangars by both Charlie and Delta companies. The troops exhibited exceptional valour and dogged determination, and despite heavy casualties, captured both these features by 0400 hours on 29th June. There was heavy resistance from Saddle. However, Delta Company was able to capture it by 0700 hours on 29th June, supported by direct fire from Bofors. The enemy lost heart and fled, leaving behind their dead and a huge quantity of arms and ammunition.

## Complex Captured (Point 4700)

MAP 10: Capture of Point 4700 Complex

Having put the enemy off balance, the plan for Phase II of the operation was modified to take the greatest advantage of the situation. A bold decision was taken to capture Rocky and Sangar, simultaneously, by day, with direct fire support from Bofors. H Hour was set at 1700 hours. The enemy was taken entirely by surprise and fled. The objectives were captured by 1930 hours on 29th June.

To maintain the momentum of the operation, Bravo Company was launched to capture the strategic Junction Point area on 1st July. It was captured by 0300 hours on the next day, without a single casualty.

# The Taming of Tiger Hill

After the battle of Tololing and the successful attack on Hump, 18 GREN was given the task of capturing Tiger Hill on 26th June. The Grenadiers, also nicknamed 'The Pole Star Battalion', had been tested by fire and had already lost two of their valiant officers, Lt Col R. Vishwanathan, its second-in-command, and Major Rajesh Adhikari. However, they had by now become battle-hardened and were determined to succeed. Before they took on the task of Tiger Hill, they had had a few days of rest and refit, wherein they honed their newly learned skills, and refined their tactics to deal with an enemy perched on high mountain features.

Colonel Khushal Thakur, CO 18 GREN, had also demanded and got adequate time for reconnaissance. His second in command and Company Commanders stayed out for five days and four nights to learn all they could about the terrain and the disposition of the enemy. They were also provided with aerial reconnaissance photographs and given valuable information about the enemy by 8 SIKH who had been in contact with the enemy since the beginning of the war.

The draft plan was made on 2nd July and it was decided that the southern approach was the most likely one to succeed, despite anticipating stiff opposition from the enemy. It was also appreciated that the majority of the enemy's weapons were deployed to cover the southern and western approaches. The western approach consisted of five military-named features from the peak of Tiger Hill—Top, Collar, India Gate, Helmet and Rocky Knob. The western approach was used by the enemy for their logistics and supply chain, and they were deployed all along this spur.

The eastern and northeastern approaches were steep and difficult to climb but, at the same time, surprise could only be achieved through these. The enemy deployment was also considered to be minimal along these approaches. Applying the lessons learnt earlier at Tololing and Hump, Colonel Khushal Thakur decided on a multidirectional attack, with the majority of the force level assaulting from an unexpected direction.

The plan thus finalized was that all four companies would initially move up along the southern spur. Two kilometres short of Tiger Hill's top, the Ghatak platoon led by Lt Balwan, and Charlie Company led by Major Joy Dasgupta, would peel off and

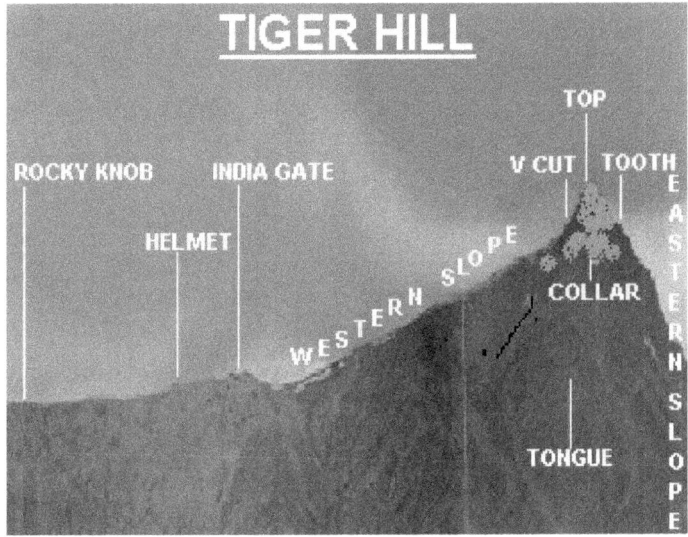

MAP 11: Tiger Hill Features

assault from the northeastern direction by almost going behind the enemy.

Delta Company, commanded by Major Sachin Nimbalkar, was to assault from the east, while Alpha Company was to engage the enemy from the south, thereby giving the impression to the enemy that the assault was coming from this direction. Bravo Company was placed in reserve.

The surprise and deception factor is crucial to success, and it played a vital role in the eventual outcome of the battle. However, an incident had taken place before the attack, which had the potential to jeopardize the surprise element and result in failure with a heavy cost—the lives of men. At the time, the visual and print media were on overdrive, reporting the war live to drawing rooms all over India. One of them, then a greenhorn TV journalist, decided to take footage of the Bofors gun shooting directly at Tiger Hill, and televised it shortly thereafter.

This had two effects. Firstly, the location of the gun was exposed and it became a target of counter-bombardment by the enemy, and had to be shifted. Secondly, it gave away the surprise by announcing the assault to the enemy, with a bang! Now, the enemy would be ready to take us on.

Whether the enemy guessed it or not is a matter of speculation, but later it was revealed that the Pakistani Post Commander at Tiger Hill had left for his administrative base on the other side of the LOC. He was intercepted later, when he was hurriedly returning on the day of the actual attack. He managed to reach his post just in the nick of time. Perhaps he returned due to this alert created by the direct broadcast on the television channels.

On 1st July, General V.P. Malik, the Chief of the Army Staff (COAS), enquired of Lieutenant General Krishan Pal, the Corps Commander, whether the attack had been launched. When he replied in the negative, General Malik asked him to switch his

TV set on and see the live telecast for himself!* On ground, the attack was still a few days away.

~

The attacking columns began their advance only on 3rd July at 2030 hours. Prior to this, Tiger Hill was subjected to thirty minutes of intense artillery shelling by 120 guns, including Bofors guns and multi-barrel rocket launchers. The sight of the shells striking home gladdened the hearts of the assaulting troops, and steeled their resolve to capture Tiger Hill.

The weather was inclement, but that helped in the element of surprise. The rain and snow in the higher reaches had reduced visibility, and this enabled the movement of attacking troops to go undetected. The enemy only detected the move when Alpha Company was barely 100 metres short of the objective, on the southern spur. They thought that the assault was building up from this direction and, therefore, concentrated their entire attention to meet this challenge. Alpha Company suffered one fatal casualty and four to five were injured.

During this time, Major Sachin Nimbalkar led his company in scaling the formidable peak from the eastern direction. In the absence of a path that led upwards, these brave men climbed a feature that would challenge the skills of any trained mountaineer—amidst the barrage of enemy artillery fire, in complete darkness and in foul weather. The men were tired. They were also uncertain about the sort of enemy opposition they would face on the top. To ensure surprise, they moved in complete silence throughout the climb.

To their good fortune, at the Tiger Hill Top, the leading scouts found that the sangars in view were not occupied by the enemy—they were busy looking for them in another direction! The attack plan had worked perfectly, and the enemy was still

---

* Narrated to me by Lt. Gen. Krishan Pal in a personal interaction.

concentrating on engaging Alpha Company, which was climbing up the southern spur. After around fifteen minutes, Lt Balwan and the Ghataks had climbed up on ropes and reached the Top. Major Nimbalkar was overjoyed to see his fellow officer, and relayed the news to the Commanding Officer: 'Tiger Hill Top is ours, sir!' The joy of making it to the top was so much that for a moment they'd even forgotten the presence of the enemy in the sangars on the other side! They immediately gathered themselves and set course to meet the challenge.

It was now three hours past midnight. The two companies sandwiched the enemy troops, who were in seven to eight sangars, connected by a communication trench* that ran along the entire ridgeline. Despite the complete surprise of the movement of these two companies, the enemy put up a very stiff resistance. Finally, the determination of our soldiers paid off and the intruders ran away, leaving behind ten of their fallen comrades. The Top was under our control and our soldiers quickly occupied the hastily evacuated sangars.

However, the situation was far from stable, and the battle was still not over, as the enemy entrenched in the Collar feature was still firing very heavily upon our troops. Throughout that day, it was an eyeball-to-eyeball conflict, as the two sides were separated by a distance of only 30–40 yards. No further progress ahead could be made during the daylight hours, as that would have been suicidal.

After last light on the night of 4$^{th}$ July, the Ghataks of Grenadiers planned an attack on Collar. Although the Top was separated from Collar by only thirty or forty yards, there was a Saddle in between, which meant that the assaulting troops would have to go down and then rush upwards to the enemy bunkers. The Grenadiers carried out the frontal assault, but a

---

* A communication trench is dug between firing trenches and bunkers/sangars to allow soldiers to move about even while the artillery is firing.

heavy and lethal volley of fire cut down the attacking troops.

Finally the attack was halted, but not before losing the lives of seven Ghataks.

Grenadier Yogendra Singh Yadav was one of the leading scouts of the assaulting Ghataks. While he was moving towards the enemy sangars, he felt a burst of UMG fire tear into his legs and abdomen. Unmindful of his injuries, he continued to fire at the enemy till his ammunition ran out. He lay unconscious amongst the others who were dead.

The enemy came and sprayed bullets once again on these fallen bravehearts. Yogendra Singh came to his senses and felt him being kicked in the abdomen. He continued to lie doggo,* until the enemy went back. It was now time for him to return, and make sure that he conveyed the fate of the others to his colleagues. He continued his journey, crawling slowly. It took him ages, seemingly, to reach the safety of his unit, and narrate the incident. Grenadier Yogendra Singh Yadav was later awarded Param Vir Chakra for the highest act of gallantry.

Although the enemy's attack had not succeeded, our soldiers vowed to avenge their losses. After reaching Tiger Hill Top, further progress by 18 GREN was difficult, as the enemy was firmly entrenched in the Collar and continued to fire. This resulted in a standoff.

Realizing this, Brigadier Bajwa, the Brigade Commander ordered 8 SIKH, who had been on Tiger Hill for a long time now, to try and cut off the western approach that was being used by the enemy for reinforcements. To carry out this task, 8 SIKH created an ad-hoc company consisting of men pooled in from different companies. Major Ravindra Panwar, the Delta Company Commander, was to lead four JCOs and fifty-two soldiers, along with Lt R.K. Sehrawat as his second in command.

Initially, the Brigade Commander had planned for this ad-

---

* To keep still and hide/remain unnoticed.

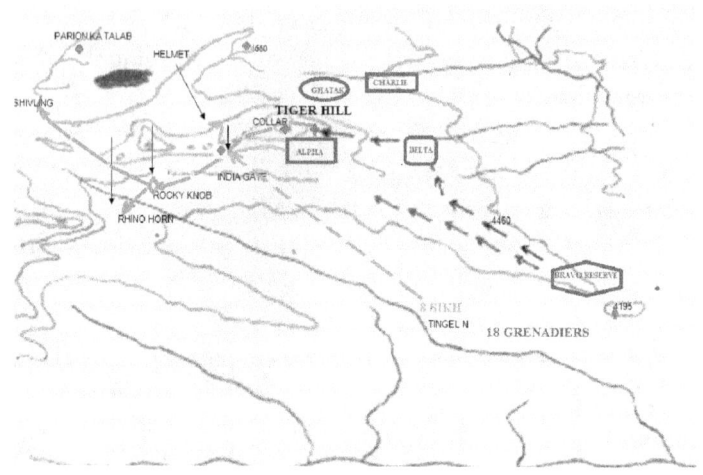

MAP 12: Battle of Tiger Hill

hoc company to simulate an attack on the western spur, to divert and deceive the enemy. However, Major Ravindra insisted that, instead of simply simulating a feigned attack, his company would actually try and dislodge the enemy and gain a foothold on the spur. He was raring to go. He had his way and was told to execute his plan.

On 4th July, this company advanced during the day, and by 2000 hours, had reached the base of the western spur. Heavy rain and fog at night helped them to move undetected. Throughout this time, total radio silence and secrecy was maintained to ensure that the move would be a surprise. This was contrary to the orders of the higher headquarters, as they needed to have intimate control of the battle, but Major Ravindra persisted, and had his way, yet again.

From the base upwards, the climb was very steep and the company could not have moved together. Thus, a small team under Lt Sehrawat, including three JCOs, went in advance. While moving up, Lt Sehrawat sprained his ankle, but he would

War trophy

View of frozen Zoji La

View of Batalik

Helicopter on a Ladakh range ridgeline

Reading letters on the battlefield

Soldiers of 17 JAT after a victory at Mashkoh

Captain Vikrant Desai, the first patrol leader to encounter the intruders

Lt Surve and his men at Sando post

Major Sonam with the author

Officers and soldiers, 8 SIKH

18 GRENADIERS at the base of Tololing

Col M.B. Ravindranath, CO, 2 RAJ RIFLES, and his men at the top of Tololing, after its capture

JAK RIF, Captain Vikram Batra's battalion

Troops at the LoC

The victorious Ladakh Scouts

Kargil Conference, Monterey, California, 2002

not hear of going down or being evacuated. He ordered his men to continue the advance without fussing over him and despite the ankle, moved forward himself.

On the morning of 5th July at 0300 hours, when they were 100 metres short of the feature India Gate, the Pakistanis opened fire. However, when our troops fired back with rocket launchers and LMG, the enemy ran away. This small group of men quickly rushed up and occupied the stone sangars left behind by the enemy. The two features of India Gate and Helmet were captured.

Dawn brought artillery fire, airburst shells, and accurate and effective enemy fire. Due to this, the rest of the company could not move up, and Sehrawat was cut off, along with twenty men. Throughout the day these brave men, isolated from their company, endured relentless artillery fire and were forced to crawl under rocks and boulders in search of shelter from the deadly shell splinters. Despite such heavy fire, they managed to cut the Pakistani telephone line which connected Tiger Hill to Rocky Knob.

After last light on 5th July, Major Ravindra managed to join up with his company under the cover of darkness. Thereafter, the defences of the company were organized and the men were told to find shelter wherever they could. These men had the enemy on both sides: at Collar and Rocky Knob. This meant that they could be attacked from either, or even both, of these directions.

Around midnight, Colonel S.P. Singh, CO 8 SIKH, spoke to Major Ravindra and told him that according to information received from higher headquarters, the enemy on Tiger Hill was desperate and a counter-attack was imminent. He asked Major Ravindra whether they would be able to hold on, and the reply he got was, 'We will remain here, come what may, or 8 Sikh will repeat Saragarhi!' He was referring to the famous battle of Saragarhi in which a complete post consisting of twenty-two Sikh troops chose to die fighting, rather than surrender, defending their post against thousands of Pathan tribesmen.

This company then waited, very sure that daylight would bring the enemy baying for their blood. The temperature was still below zero, they had no shelter, and they could not afford to sleep. They were numb with cold as they watched the stars disappear.

As dawn broke on 6th July at 0600 hours, the enemy opened with very heavy fire. After the artillery barrage lifted, about twenty Pakistanis launched their first attack. The previous day they had seen the small number of Sehrawat's troops deployed on top, and were under the impression that the Indian presence was small. The attacking enemy got the shock of their lives when they realized that they had vastly underestimated the strength of these men. Despite that, the battle was intensely fought. Lt Sehrawat received a splinter wound in his leg, but he refused to be evacuated and continued to rally his men to repel the attack. Subedar Nirmal Singh played a key role in motivating and inspiring the men to counter the attack. Finally, the attackers were pushed back, though at the cost of a few casualties.

Before Major Ravindra had time to assess the damage, evacuate the dead and the wounded, and reorganize his defences, the enemy launched yet another attack. This time, around forty to forty-five Pakistanis charged, screaming down the Rocky Knob feature from two different directions. What followed was an hour of brutal savagery as only brave men are capable of. Fierce hand-to-hand fighting ensued, and the cries of the injured and the dying filled the desolate and barren land.

The Khalsas fought like lions and were valiantly led by the two officers. Major Ravindra picked up a light machine gun from a wounded man and killed four enemy soldiers. Even after receiving a bullet wound in his left leg, he kept firing and inspired his men.

At the end of this carnage, victory was ours and the enemy

ran away, leaving behind the dead, yet again. They had suffered heavy casualties, and the bodies of two of their officers, namely, Major Iqbal and Captain Karnal Sher Khan,* along with thirty of their men, lay strewn around. A large number of enemy soldiers had also sustained casualties and fallen into the nala, about 100 metres below.

The brave fight offered by Captain Karnal Sher Khan is worthy of admiration; as fellow soldiers, our troops did have a word of praise for him. He was awarded the 'Nishan-e-Haider' later, the Pakistani equivalent of the Param Vir Chakra, a tacit indication that the intruders were none but Pakistani Army soldiers. He belonged to the 27th Sindh Regiment in the Pakistan Army and was sent to 12 Northern Light Infantry (12 NLI) for Operations in Kargil, code-named Koh-e-Paima (Operation KP).†

By 0900 hours, the situation had stabilized. Victory was achieved, but at a very high cost, with three JCOs and fourteen other ranks dead, and two officers and eighteen other ranks badly injured. However, this company tried to reorganize itself as best it could for it was left with only twenty fighting men. There could not be any casualty evacuation, and the wounded were given whatever first-aid was available in situ.

Colonel S.P. Singh spoke to his men after this attack to inspire them; he said to them that he was proud of them. While he was talking on the radio to injured Lt Sehrawat, the three nights and days of battle finally caught up with this brave young man. He broke down and cried, saying that his men were dead, and that he was the commander of these men who died in front of his eyes. He was in a critical condition and was barely able to speak. The

---

* https://en.wikipedia.org/wiki/Karnal_Sher_Khan; accessed on 25 January 2019.

† Zehra, Naseem, 'From Kargil to the Coup: Events that Shook Pakistan' also known as 'Op Badr.' www.bookmaza.com

Colonel consoled him the best he could and the conscientious young soldier felt stronger.

The company waited for the next counter-attack and the next round of fighting, with gritted teeth. There were no further enemy attacks that day.

~

This counter-attack and its subsequent failure was the most important and decisive part of the battle of Tiger Hill. If Major Ravindra's company had not been able to gain a foothold at the India Gate feature and thus cut off the reinforcement route for the troops who were in the Collar feature, then the battle could have swung either way. To break the standoff which was faced by 18 GREN, it was important to isolate the enemy entrenched in the Collar feature. 8 SIKH not only succeeded in doing that, but they also killed the two officers who were leading the company deployed on Tiger Hill, thus breaking the will of the enemy to fight.

Realizing that the strength of Major Ravindra's company was too little to ward off another attack, the second-in-command of 8 SIKH, Major Dalbir Singh took two JCOs and eighteen other soldiers to reinforce it. They moved in broad daylight, despite the intense artillery fire. They suffered one fatal casualty en route, but reached the casualty-stricken company by 2230 hours via the southern approach. Thereafter, the company was re-deployed to counter the threat of another attack.

At first light on 7th July, the Company Commander and those of the wounded who could walk, numbering two officers and 18 others, were sent back to HQ for medical aid. The dead were shifted to an appropriate place, and the feature was held by approximately forty men. Until 8th July, the situation remained unchanged as the expected attack by the enemy did not come.

Meanwhile, enemy artillery fire continued to harass this company, resulting in a few splinter injuries as there was no overhead protection. Our artillery was, meanwhile, engaging the Rocky Knob feature. After last light on 8th July, 18 GREN resumed their operations and moved up more of their men to finally launch an offensive to clear the Tiger Hill feature completely.

~

Assuming that Tiger Hill and Area Collar were clear of the enemy threat from these directions, Major Dalbir turned his attention towards Rocky Knob, the feature from where the enemy had launched two counter-attacks. He requested for permission to exploit the situation, and launched an attack on Rocky Knob. To facilitate his attack, an artillery barrage was fired upon Rocky Knob at 0430 hours on 8th July. After an hour of artillery shelling, 8 SIKH launched their attack towards Rocky Knob, which was 200 metres away from Helmet.

As the assaulting troops went in, they were surprised by a heavy volume of effective and accurate fire coming towards them from Tiger Hill. To their horror, they realized that the enemy that had been previously entrenched on Tiger Hill Top had now moved down to the Collar area and was still hiding in the rocks there. 18 GREN had still not completed their mopping-up operations and it was this band of isolated enemy soldiers who were firing at them. Under such heavy fire from behind, the attack petered out and could not progress further until the enemy troops located in the Collar area were eliminated.

18 GREN planned an operation for the Collar on 8th July. Alpha Company was still on the southern spur, pinned down by enemy fire and unable to move. Hence, for this operation, one company was sent from the eastern direction and the assault was launched on the same evening. After the failure of the counter-attacks on 8 SIKH earlier, the enemy was disheartened. They panicked, and started fleeing. But the Grenadiers recalled their vow to avenge their losses, and shot them dead. Approximately

fifteen enemy soldiers were killed; five bodies were recovered intact, others lay in irretrievable locations in deep gorges. Our own casualties were minimal, mainly caused by splinters from enemy artillery shelling.

After consolidating and mopping up the Collar feature, 18 GREN then linked up with the company of 8 SIKH which was holding India Gate and Helmet. Since this company had suffered heavy casualties in the three days of continuous intense fighting, the task of continuing the operations was given to 18 GREN.

After receiving the information about enemy disposition from the 8 SIKH company, the Grenadiers launched an attack on Rocky Knob on 10$^{th}$ July. Though they did not face much enemy resistance, they did come across lot of anti-personnel mines strewn en route, left by the fleeing enemy. They killed one of the enemy snipers and recovered a large quantity of arms and ammunition.

To exploit the situation further, the Grenadiers pushed on further, and captured the features Rhino Horn, Shivling and Point 4965, without encountering any enemy resistance. The entire Tiger Hill feature was free of the enemy, who had left behind their dead, along with vast quantities of arms and ammunition.

At last, Tiger Hill was tamed and the battle there was over!

# Fall of Grand Mashkoh Hub

## Point 4875

Point 4875 in Mashkoh, at a height of more than 16,000 feet, is a towering mountain peak which is visible from the National Highway. Therefore any position on it occupied by the enemy can also be used to observe and bring down fire on our military convoys. Although it had turned out to be the hub of their defence and logistical activities, the area had not been given priority earlier, as it lay back from the highway and significant enemy activities had initially not been discovered there. It was now clear that our troops had to remove the enemy from there at the earliest.

The mountain features are given names generally keeping in mind their appearance or resemblance to something else, to make it easy to identify them. The Point 4875 Complex consisted of several small peaks named Whale Back, Twin Pimples, Twin Bumps, Rocky Knob, Hump and Tip.

Since the capture of Point 4875 was crucial to the success of the 79 Mountain Brigade's operations under Brigadier R.K. Kakar, a large number of planning parametres were taken into consideration. Adequate time was available to go into minute details, unlike the earlier operations. After positioning troops around the objectives earlier, the final attack was planned for commencement on the night of 4$^{th}$ July.

To achieve surprise, it was decided to attack the enemy

from the direction they would consider least likely. As attacking straight upwards under the enemy's observation was considered suicidal, this approach was finalized to launch the attack. Two brigade-sized firm bases, meant to provide a launching pad to the assaulting troops, were established by the reserve battalion to confuse the enemy about the direction of the assault. Further, each objective was to be attacked adopting a multi-directional approach. Accordingly, two battalions with two companies each were to simultaneously contact the enemy's main defences at Point 4875 and Pimple complexes.

A block was established towards the enemy's likely escape route in Safaid Nala to prevent enemy troops from falling back to defended localities. This, along with the establishment of fire bases would effectively prevent any reinforcements to the whole Point 4875 complex, thereby isolating it. By now the effectiveness of direct artillery fire by Bofors was proven; therefore, it was deployed in the same role to cause maximum attrition of the enemy defences.

17 JAT was assigned to capture Pimple I and Whale Back. After a stealthy climb lasting the whole night, they attacked early in the morning, even before dawn, under Major R.K. Singh and Major Deepak Rampal.

The attack initially worked according to the plan. The enemy continued to resist with heavy fire from all types of weapons and made progress very difficult, but the attacking columns didn't allow them to gain the upper hand and persisted resolutely. Fierce fighting on the objective, including hand-to-hand close combat, went on for some time before the enemy was pushed back from Pimple I and Whale Back. But, before the troops could get reorganized at Whale Back, the enemy came back to counter-attack. Major Rampal immediately asked for artillery support and for the battalion's supporting weapons to switch fire towards his direction. He was able to repulse the counter-attack launched by the enemy, but it was not yet the time to relax and recoup. He completed his reorganization quickly and replenished his

*Fall of Grand Mashkoh Hub* 111

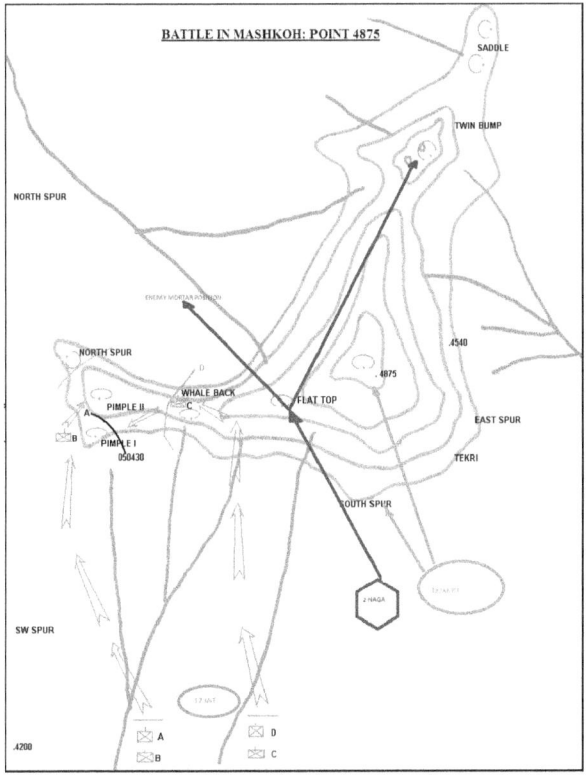

MAP 13: Battle of Mashkoh

ammunition from the stock which had come up with the reserve troops following them. His prompt and determined actions came in handy, and two more counter-attacks from the enemy were successfully repulsed on the same day.

~

While this operation developed, a similarly intense battle was being fought by 13 JAK RIF, which had been assigned other two objectives: Point 4875 and South Spur. Two company commanders, Majors S.V. Bhaskar and Gurpreet Singh, led their

Alpha and Charlie companies towards their objectives. Alpha Company reached east of the enemy at Point 4875, while Charlie Company managed to consolidate at South Spur, and moved towards area Flat Top which was west of Point 4875, towards Whale Back, in the middle of the two localities. The enemy was firing heavily from the bunkers at both the strongholds. It made further movement very difficult. The attack was stalled and, to make matters worse, daylight had broken, so the enemy was able to see the soldiers and shoot at them.

We cannot underestimate the power of a single man; most of the times, he tips the scales. The exceptional bravery of a simple village lad, Sanjay Kumar, turned the battle in favour of not only his battalion, but also his motherland. It is heartening to learn about Sanjay Kumar's grit and determination, despite facing failures earlier in life. He is the youngest among six children. His two elder brothers were in ITBP and one of his uncles had served in the J&K Rifles and was martyred in the 1965 Indo-Pak War. He had resolved to join the same regiment. He attempted to join the Army twice, as a recruit, but could not make it. He came to Delhi to look for a job and learnt driving, but returned to his native Himachal, where he became a taxi-driver in Bilaspur. He, however, did not lose his determination and will to join the Indian Army as a soldier. His third attempt at Jabalpur made him a soldier, at last. Who could have known then that Sanjay Kumar would later be known for his legendary bravery?

As the attack on Point 4875 had stalled due to heavy enemy fire from one of the bunkers in area Flat Top, Sepoy Sanjay Kumar, a volunteer leading scout, inched forward. One of the enemy bunkers at Flat Top spewed out bullets from a UMG. He was not deterred, and charged towards that bunker through a hail of enemy bullets. With exceptional courage and bravery, he continued his ferocious assault on the bunker, despite being hit twice in the chest, and killed a couple of enemy soldiers. He then rushed towards the next bunker from where the enemy was firing the machine gun. The enemy fled, leaving behind the machine gun with the ammunition loaded in it. Sanjay turned the gun towards the fleeing enemy and shot many of them down, lest they return to counter-attack later. He refused to be evacuated until the complete area was cleared of the enemy.

The battle for South Spur was over, with a bonus—the capture of area Flat Top, which was supposed to happen later, as per the plans. At this point of time, the company advancing towards Point 4875 was still in a firefight with the enemy and was unable to advance due to being caught in the daylight. However now, with Flat Top in the hands of our own troops, the enemy was boxed in from three directions: east, west and south.

Taking quick advantage of the position gained by them, both the companies pushed towards Point 4875 and, a little after midday, they were able to capture it. With the fall of Point 4875, a major victory was achieved by our troops in the Mashkoh area. However, the enemy was still holding out at many places and the second phase of the brigade's plan needed to be launched.

## Pimple II, Twin Bumps and Ledge in Mashkoh

In the second phase of operations, 17 JAT was to capture Pimple II. Since Flat Top was already taken by 13 JAK RIF, it was to remain a reserve battalion. The 2nd Battalion of the Naga Regiment (2 NAGA) had come into the battlefield and was employed to capture Twin Bumps.

17 JAT decided to launch the attack on the next night, from the direction of Whale Back. During the initial advance, Major Ritesh Sharma, the commander of Bravo Company, sustained splinter injuries and started to bleed profusely, necessitating evacuation to the nearest medical post. The reins of the company fell upon the young shoulders of Captain Anuj Nayyar, its second-in-command. After a brief pause, he led his company from the front and, despite heavy artillery, mortars and automatic fire, he

kept motivating his command to continue the advance towards Pimple II. However, due to stiff resistance, progress was slower than expected.

Captain Nayyar fought bravely through the day, and made a final, successful dash towards the objective. There, he located four well-concealed enemy bunkers, which were attacking our troops with automatic machine guns. He deployed his rocket launcher detachment and took two of his men from the leading section with him as he crawled ahead. Bullets were whizzing past him but he was not deterred. He lobbed the hand grenade into the first bunker and silenced it.

Without halting, Captain Nayyar now rushed towards the second bunker and managed to lob another grenade into it as well. With a blast, smoke emerged from inside the bunker. He saw the clothing of a few escaping enemy soldiers catch fire. The other two bunkers had been continuously firing at him, but by now one of his platoons had taken position from where they could support him.

The third bunker fell when he, along with some of his men, rushed and cleared it. The last bunker remained and the enemy seemed determined not to run away. It seems the enemy had by then spotted him and realized that he must be the leader who was causing all the havoc. Usually, a rocket launcher is used against a bunker or a tank, but the enemy decided to fire it at Captain Nayyar directly. The rocket hit him on the head and he succumbed to his injuries.

Captain Anuj Nayyar had studied in Army Public School, New Delhi and had joined the battalion just two years earlier. But in his short duration with the battalion, he had endeared himself immensely to the troops under his command. During his hours on the battlefield, he had killed nine enemy soldiers and destroyed three MMG bunkers, as well as capturing dozens of enemy weapons. He was awarded the Maha Vir Chakra for his gallant act.

Due to the loss of their leader, the troops were asked to pull back to safety, but not before recovering his dead body and the weapons he had captured. Pimple II was still not in hand. However, 2 NAGA had made steady progress and captured Twin Bumps by midday the next day, after heavy fighting.

## Ledge Invites Wrath

A small group of enemy soldiers on a very narrow ledge extending northwards from Point 4875 had not been noticed before. They were effectively interfering in any movement towards Pimple II. The enemy needed to be cleared from this location for the victory to be complete.

Major Vohra reinforced the troops at Point 4875, along with Captain Vikram Batra and his company. Firefighting continued all through the next day. A sangar on the ledge was creating the most hindrance. Captain Naveen proceeded to charge at the sangar, but was injured in a grenade blast.

Captain Vikram Batra was with him. He took charge of the situation, gathered his men and rushed towards the sangar, killing all five enemy soldiers inside it. Just when he thought the battle was over and was calling over the rest of his men, he was hit first by a bullet in his chest and then a rocket that seemed to have come out of nowhere. He succumbed to his injuries on the spot.

The situation turned grave once again. An injured Major Vohra took stock. When he was proceeding to assault the narrow ledge, he was voluntarily joined by Major D Faujdar, who had come up as the artillery support commander. The ledge once again echoed with the battle cries of our soldiers and, seeing their fury, the enemy fled, leaving behind dozens of their dead, a large number of weapons and a huge quantity of ammunition. Major Vohra called up on his radio set and yelled 'NAPOLEON!', the success signal for the capture of the ledge.

17 JAT was finally able to capture Pimple II, once the ledge was in our hands.

~

The enemy launched well-coordinated counter-attacks in the next 48 hours on all the locations, including Pimple II and Twin Bumps. These counter-attacks were repulsed by coordinated small arms and artillery fire, with heavy casualties to the enemy.

A day later, patrols of 2 NAGA located an enemy mortar position which was playing havoc with our troops and launched a raid on it. Sepoy Imliakum Ao displayed exemplary courage, grit and determination during the raid. He directly charged the enemy sentries and killed both of them, paving the way for the capture of the enemy's mortars. Their mortar position was destroyed. Sepoy Imliakum Ao was awarded the Maha Vir Chakra for his gallant act. In the next two days, 2 NAGA captured Rocky Knob, Hump and Tips.

~

In the operation in Mashkoh, the enemy suffered a large number of casualties, as was evident from the number of dead bodies left behind. In a rare honour, and for the first time in the history of the Indian Army, two Param Vir Chakras were awarded in this sector, that too in a single battle, by the same battalion, 13 JAK RIF, for exceptional bravery: to Captain Vikram Batra of 'Dil maange more' fame and Rifleman Sanjay Kumar. The battle beyond the Point 4875 complex and the advance towards the LOC continued thereafter until the complete area was cleared of the enemy, and the LOC restored.

# Part IV

## Battles at Batalik-Yaldor—Chorbat La—Turtok—Siachen

# Operations in Batalik-Yaldor

The area around Batalik, right up to Junk Lungpa is known as Yaldor. The LOC is towards the north and the mighty Indus flows along its southern portion and enters POK, near Batalik. Like the Tiger Hill in Dras, Shangruti is an imposing mountain peak running east-west. The top was held by the enemy. From the top, a ridgeline runs southwards with Bump I, Bump II, and bifurcating at Bump III into two ridges, Jubar and Kukarthang-Tharu, and terminates at the Indus River. The other ridge in the area is the Khalubar-Stangba ridge which originates from the LOC area and runs between Gragriobar and Junk Lungpa nalas. At the extreme east lie the Churubar Sispo and Gonpathang ridgelines, which separate Yaldor from an area locally known as Chorbat La.

The entire area around Batalik is very rugged and has steep razor-sharp ridges, offering no place to create a camp. Besides a few mountain tracks used by the locals, no other movement is possible, except along the Indus. This is where the encounters and heroic exploits of Captain Desai and Lt Surve took place (see 'Detection of Intrusion and Initial Response'). The last leg of the war took shape here as well.

Several smaller actions, such as patrolling and sending small ambush parties, had occurred. Once it was clear that the enemy was present in larger numbers, it was evident that a greater number of troops would be needed. It took time to travel through the most difficult terrain, and then acclimatize. Some

## YALDOR SUB SECTOR

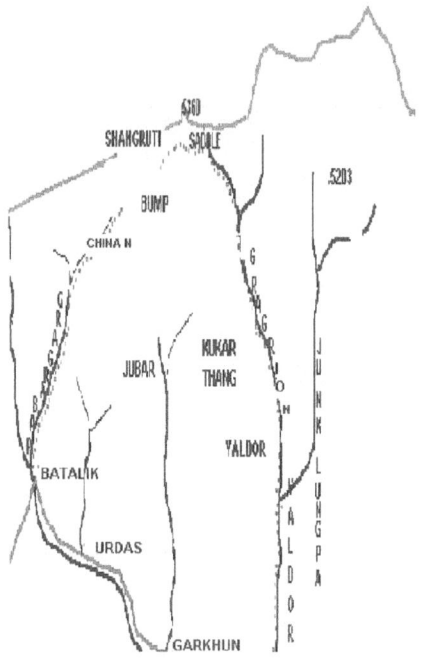

MAP 14: Yaldor Sub-sector

troops were launched straight into action, without waiting for too long, as prompt operation before the enemy could find* their feet was paramount. As the area is difficult to reach, most of the war reporting about it was done from Dras and other places.

An infantry brigade under Brigadier Devinder Singh was mustered up by the end of the first week of May 1999. While the troops arrived, assessing the enemy location was crucial to plan the operations ahead. From the reports by the patrols and other parties, it was ascertained that the enemy had occupied

---

* A fighting unit/sub-unit firms up in the battlefield by rearranging themselves to use the available ground for protection and cover from enemy fire, thus staying in position.

*Operations in Batalik-Yaldor* 121

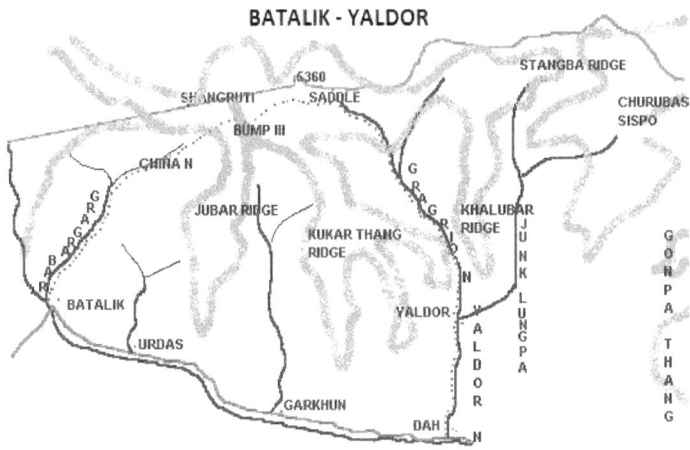

MAP 15: Batalik-Yaldor

several mountain features and heights on and around Jubar and Kukarthang ridgelines. It was initially felt that not more than twenty to thirty enemy soldiers at each location could be sustained in such a terrain, so the plan was made accordingly. The first thing to do was to prevent the enemy from coming further up and occupying more peaks. The main idea, thereafter, was to block the routes of enemy sustenance from the western flank, and clear off the intrusion from the south and southeast. For this, it was important to capture the junction of all the above ridgelines at Bump III, short of a mountain peak near the LOC, Shangruti. There were two more Bumps in between (See Map 18). Intrusion at other places, such as Khalubar, was also to be tackled simultaneously, depending upon the availability of troops.

Our troops started operating before the beginning of the third week of May 1999. Thanks to a daredevil act by the Para Special Forces, a foothold was established near Bump II in the initial stages itself. This was a great advantage, as the enemy had not occupied it yet, nor had they realized the presence of our men.

They were seen queuing up for their meals nearby, unmindful of our presence. Unfortunately, in the excitement, one of the men pressed the trigger of his rifle. With its sharp bang, the presence of our men was announced. The enemy took position and started retaliation immediately. They brought down heavy fire with all the weapons they had been able to muster, and gathered men to assault the foothold.

This foothold needed to be reinforced but, unfortunately, no link from the south was possible in such a short time frame. The foothold was abandoned within a few days. In hindsight, had it been possible to stay on there, the enemy would not have got a chance to take over these ridgelines later on and establish themselves.

A similar move was envisaged from the east of Yaldor Nala, to block the enemy's route of maintenance and subsequent link up with Bump II. Once the enemy was completely isolated, mopping up could be carried out from different directions, one location at a time. The nearest battalions that could be spared were 1/11 Gorkha Rifles (1/11 GR) under officiating CO Lt Col Asthana, and 12 Jammu & Kashmir Light Infantry (12 JAK LI). The battalions were on their way to peace stations after completing their tenure in Siachen; a large number of men had already left as the advance party, and many were on leave.

One of the first tasks given to 1/11 GR was to contain the situation in Yaldor. 1/11 GR launched operations to capture Point 4821 on Kukarthang ridge, and reached a few hundred metres short of the objective, from the northeast. They were also able to contact and retrieve Captain Vikrant Desai and his team, who had been unable to extricate themselves for the last eight to ten days (see 'Detection of Intrusion and Initial Response'). The enemy was in full strength by now. No further progress was possible on this ridgeline for some time to come.

Similarly, 12 JAK LI, commanded by Col V.S. Bhalotia, attempted to press along Gragrio Bar, but drew heavy fire from the western slopes of Khalubar and another nearby peak. Consequently, the plan was slightly modified, and it was decided they would advance up to Khalubar ridge from Yaldor Nala. A company was sent along Junk Lungpa to secure the eastern flank. The battalion captured several places on the Bharkar Ridgeline, but the attempts to capture Point 4812 did not succeed.

Some modification of the initial plan was carried out for the eastern flank operations. It was decided to advance along Junk Lungpa to threaten the enemy's line of maintenance, west of Khalubar-Stangba ridge. But the operations on this flank still suffered setbacks, as the enemy soldiers on Point 5203 interfered. It seemed to be occupied by a large number of troops. The movement along Junk Lungpa Nala was also affected. A plan had to be made to capture Point 5203, which was launched on 7$^{th}$ June and, after initial success, took another two weeks' time before its final capture. It has been subsequently covered in this book. While this was being done, the battle at the Jubar Complex was also developing.

## Battle of Jubar Complex

The 1$^{st}$ Battalion of the Bihar Regiment (1 BIHAR), under Colonel O.P. Yadav, had arrived in the third week of May. The need to contain the enemy was becoming more and more urgent by the day. All earlier attempts to capture objectives where the enemy had been sighted had not met with any success, and the local troops present had fallen back to their defences. Therefore, even before the battalion had fully arrived and settled, the CO was asked to capture the enemy's nearest observation post on the Jubar complex, the Jubar OP, at a height of 16,400 feet. He was given some additional troops that were in the area.

The first attempt by 1 BIHAR also failed, as not much planning or preparation had been possible in the rush. The troops had not even been oriented to the new location. 1 BIHAR was,

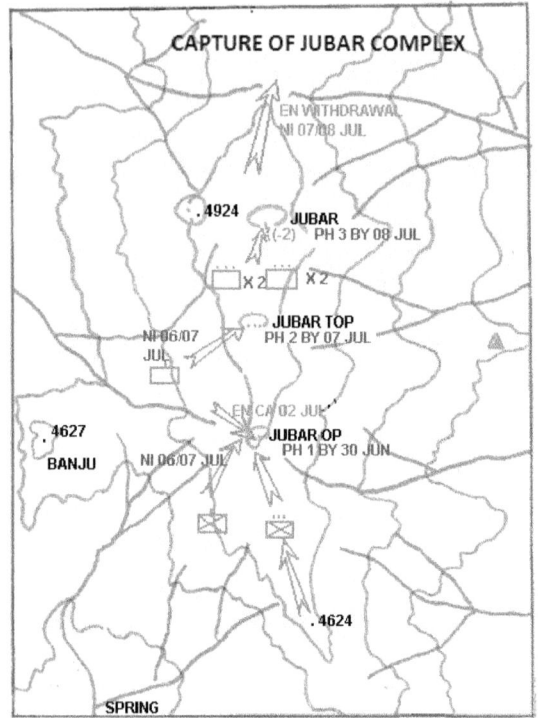

MAP 16: Capture of Jubar OP

then, tasked with containing the enemy in this area, and relieving the others.

Within a week of their arrival, an attack on Jubar Hill was launched by the Bihar battalion. Despite stiff resistance and not much artillery support, a small location near Jubar Hill was captured by the next morning. One platoon made a firm base at this point.

~

The commander of Charlie Company, Major Mariappan Sarvanan was given the task of capturing Point 4268 before the operations could proceed further—a challenge. As the success or failure of an operation depends mainly upon a good plan, ample time was now devoted to making and refining a deliberate course of action. He gathered his available troops and briefed them about the impending task and its implementation. He had planned to establish several small groups on the enemy reinforcement routes in order to curtail any movement of the enemy, inwards or outwards, i.e. 'cut-off' groups. In addition, he had planned to deploy a support group, which would be the location of all the automatic machine guns and would engage the enemy heavily. This would facilitate the capture of the enemy bunkers. While he and his men moved upwards, the artillery was to create as much destruction amongst the bunkers as possible. At the end of his briefing, he thundered that they would only breakfast the next day after capturing Point 4268. His soldiers echoed his words, and the battle cry 'Bharat Mata Ki Jai!' roared in the sky.

Charlie Company set out towards their objective during the hours of darkness. The attacking columns reached a few hundred metres short of the bunker that had been actively firing in their direction and was stalling the attack. Major Sarvanan wanted to make the most of the opportunity before daylight, a mere hour away, exposed them to danger. He picked up his radio set, called his CO and asked for illuminating rounds of artillery around the objective area so that he could see the bunkers clearly, and take an accurate aim with his rocket launcher. The CO advised him that illumination was a double-edged weapon as the enemy would also be able to see him. Major Sarvanan was confident and convinced the CO that he had already warned all his men to take cover, and not make any movement, lest they be detected.

The illuminating rounds came promptly, after a couple of minutes. Dawn was just around the corner but it appeared as though the sun had come up early for the enemy at Point 4268. Major Sarvanan took the rocket launcher from the hands of its operator and aimed at the enemy bunker that continued to vigorously pour out bullets. The rocket went through the bunker, exploding inside and splattering boulders and severed body parts everywhere! The bunker fell silent just as first light broke out. How could he have missed the opportunity? Major Sarvanan immediately cleared the area of the enemy, up till that destroyed bunker.

It was the promised breakfast time, but there was yet another bunker left to be cleared, a short distance away. It had now opened up, all guns blazing.

One of the men present, Abdullah, had been a militant in Kashmir and had once confronted Major Sarvanan in the Valley. That day, he had taken a fancy to this brave soldier. He left militancy for good, but instead of returning to Kangan, he joined the battalion without any pay or privileges! He had volunteered to shadow Major Sarvanan on the assault on Point 4268. The assaulting party lost one of their men, Naik Ganesh, early in the morning. He had been hit by a burst of machine-gun fire. Major Sarvanan had dragged him carefully behind a boulder before he collapsed. After paying his last tributes to his fallen colleague, Major Sarvanan continued crawling towards the bunker which was only a little more than a hundred feet away from him. True to his word, Abdullah was following right behind him. The next bullet grazed the major's head and blood started dripping down. He immediately tied his patka\* around his wound. In the meanwhile, the radio operator had informed the CO about the injury but, before he could get any contradictory orders, Major Sarvanan immediately convinced the CO that it was nothing serious and that he had given himself adequate first aid! The CO still asked Major Sarvanan to be cautious, and halt. He advised him to first identify where exactly the fire was coming from. In response, the major said, 'Now there is nothing that can make me halt before I capture the objective. I will only stop then to rest.' Abdullah had also advised him to halt, but Major Sarvanan

---

\* A black piece of cloth used as alternate headgear.

rebuked him, calling him a coward. He could not be stopped, neither by the hail of bullets, nor by his seniors or subordinates. Relentlessly, he progressed towards the final objective of his lifetime.

His strong will took him to just a few steps short of the bunker, despite the constant hail of bullets. Suddenly, two enemy soldiers who had remained hidden throughout, stood up, aiming at him. He got a burst of machine-gun fire directly to his head. As he fell, there was an eerie silence for a few moments, as though time had frozen; the enemy, too, stopped firing, as if to salute the brave soldier. Abdullah tried to pull him to safety, but could not do so, as the firing had resumed. Narrating this scene down below at the base, Abdullah cried inconsolably. He bitterly regretted not pulling Major Sarvanan back when he had refused to halt.

Mrs Amrita Valli Mariappan wrote a befitting tribute to Sarvanan, her son, in a simple letter to the CO. She implored all not to cry for Sarvanan as all the other soldiers who were fighting there were his brothers and therefore, her sons. Though she had lost her husband in the Indian Peace Keeping Force in Sri Lanka, and her son at Kargil, she had gained so many sons in the Indian Army. For her, 1 BIHAR had become her permanent home, to visit often and meet her sons. That's what mothers of the brave are made of.

Major Sarvanan was awarded the Vir Chakra, posthumously.

## Revety the Spiderman: Capture of Jubar OP

It was only after one month, on 29 June, that a platoon of 1 BIHAR under Captain Revety Bhandari made a fresh attempt at the Jubar OP. Revety preferred to launch a direct and frontal assault without fearing the hail of bullets, to benefit from the element of surprise. He climbed the steep rocks like Spiderman, crawling a distance of almost one kilometre. His confidence bore fruit; he was able to reach the top undetected and completely surprise the enemy. He caused heavy casualties to the occupants of the post and forced the unprepared enemy to vacate the locality.

The first thing he did after this was to reorganize his men and warn them that a counter-attack would be coming at any moment. And so it did! Thanks to his timely and bold actions, he was successful in pushing back the counter-attack to a hasty retreat. Due to his brave initiative, dogged determination and exemplary leadership, they were able to capture a vital area which acted as a firm base for the capture of the rest of the Jubar complex, the most dominant ridge in the area. This proved to be a big setback to the enemy.

While capturing the Jubar OP, the battalion suffered the loss of two brave soldiers, and nine others were injured. Captain Venkatesan Viswanathan, an Army Medical Corps officer who was the doctor available at hand, volunteered to establish a Regimental Aid Post to provide prompt treatment and evacuation of the injured soldiers. He moved up to the Jubar OP amidst heavy enemy artillery shelling and fire. His prompt treatment saved many lives.

The attack on Jubar Top was made the next night. However it was still not successful and the battalion had to establish itself on Jubar OP and the western slopes of the hill.

## Hari in a Hurry: Capture of Jubar Top

On 6$^{th}$ July, Major K.P.R. Hari attacked Jubar Top, an enemy stronghold at a height of 16,800 feet. It was a two-pronged attack under heavy enemy artillery and small arms fire. By crawling through the boulders over a steep cliff leading towards Jubar Top Major Hari managed to avoid enemy fire and reach 50 metres short of the enemy bunker. In a swift and bold manoeuvre, he closed in on the enemy bunker along with six soldiers, continuously firing and lobbing hand grenades. With utter disregard for personal safety, Major Hari destroyed the enemy's heavy machine gun bunker and killed two enemy personnel. Sensing immediate capture, the rest fled, leaving a huge quantity of arms, ammunition and equipment. The post was captured before the day broke, without any casualties.

Major K.P.R. Hari took bold actions and used his courage and determination to achieve success. His exceptional leadership in the face of extreme danger paved the way for more successes thereafter.

## Capture of Jubar Main

Along with Major K.P.R. Hari, Major Vinod Kumar Rai had been given the task of capturing the Jubar Main Complex. This included exploiting another nearby cliff, Point 4924. After the capture of Jubar Top, it was used as a launchpad for the next attack on Jubar Main.

The troops had already been fighting through the night, but there was no time to waste. Major Rai launched the attack after reorganizing his men. His party came under heavy fire as the enemy had expected them to go attack them in Jubar Main.

Movement by day under heavy observed fire is extremely dangerous. Unmindful of the hazards, Major Rai and his team continued their advance towards the objective and came across two enemy bunkers on their way. Roaring 'Bharat Mata Ki Jai!', he and his men charged towards these bunkers. Seeing their threatening pace and stance, the enemy started to run away, leaving behind their light machine guns, carbine machine guns and rifles. Some of them fell to the attackers' bullets. After the whole complex was abandoned Major Rai's troops found seven enemy soldiers' bodies lying in the area. A quick reorganization was immediately carried out to regain command and control.

By the dawn of the next day, they had been attacking the enemy for the last thirty-six hours, including two sleepless nights. They, nevertheless, did not halt as they wanted to make the most of the opportunity to capture whatever they could, while the enemy had taken to his heels. A conscious decision was taken to continue the momentum of the attack. The cliff (Point 4924) was captured in the next two hours and, finally, there was no sign of the enemy on the Jubar Complex.

## Mharo Desh: Tharu

While the above actions were underway, the enemy was holding out at the Tharu-Kukarthang Ridgeline further up, bifurcating from the Bump III area. Captain Aninder Jit Singh, a young and energetic officer, was assigned to capture Tharu with his company. He had just joined the battalion a couple of months ago. Using his training to the fullest, he launched a daring assault at night, by going behind the enemy from the north.

They were successful in surprising the enemy and were barely a few hundred metres away when they were spotted. The enemy started engaging them heavily from Tharu. Finding it difficult, Captain A.J. Singh sent a small party to his right to explore another route. They signalled that it was a possibility. Huge boulders and a steep gradient welcomed his final assault team. Only four to five men could pass through and climb up without coming under the enemy's direct observed fire.

The enemy was on the lookout for them when they finally approached the bunkers. Both the sides came face to face, suddenly. A fierce battle cry was followed by hand-to-hand fighting, but not for too long, as the enemy started escaping.

Captain A.J. Singh captured the location without suffering any injury to his own men. The rest of the area was also sanitized and found abandoned by the enemy. By 9th July, Jubar Complex and Tharu were both cleared of the enemy. Indian troops had almost reached the LOC.

# Battles on the Eastern Flank of Yaldor Area

12 JAK LI had been moving up in Junk Lungpa Nala to make an attempt on Khalubar. Heavy enemy interference was likely from farther east of Junk Lungpa, so a modification to the plan was needed. It was decided to go further east and capture the enemy's location to the east of Junk Lungpa, thereby also cutting off the enemy's line of sustenance from that direction. This modification led to the battle of Point 5203.[*]

## Battle of Point 5203

Point 5203 is a mountain peak located close to the LOC in the east of Batalik. It is a dominating feature and effectively interferes with any movement through Junk Lungpa Nala which could be used to approach it. Point 5287, a key feature on the Khalubar Ridge, which is on the opposite side of the Junk Lungpa Nala, covers the frontage of Point 5203. It was imperative to clear this point and the surrounding locations first, before developing any operations in Khalubar and Stangba. 12 JAK LI was made responsible for this operation, along with the

---

[*] Chronologically, these actions of 12 JAK LI took place before Jubar OP was captured, but for better clarity, all 1 BIHAR operations were covered simultaneously in one go earlier.

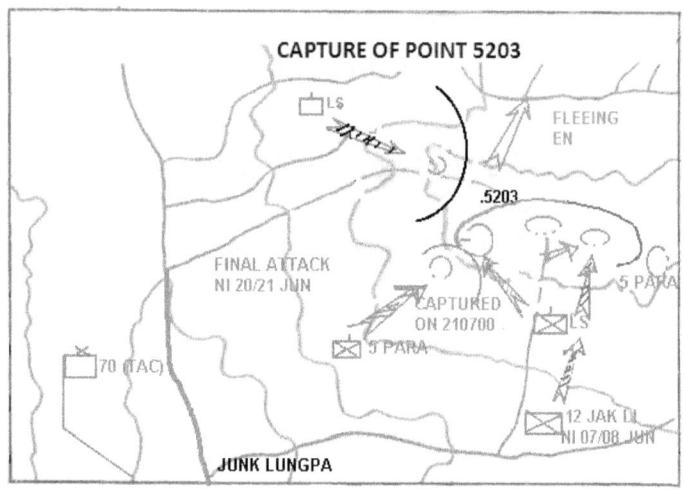

MAP 17: Capture of Point 5203

troops of 5 PARA, Ladakh Scouts and the others under the command of the battalion.

Two companies were needed to assault Point 5203, and two more as reserves. Unfortunately, not enough troops were available. Therefore, mixed troops from 12 JAK LI and 5 PARA were used in the first phase, with a simultaneous feint attack[*] on another location nearby, to distract and mislead the enemy. In the second phase, they were to clear the enemy from the rest of the localities adjacent to it.

On the night of 7$^{th}$ June two platoons, each with mixed troops, attacked Point 5203 which was a strategically important objective on the Batalik-Yaldor front. The Pakistanis had taken up strong defences there and had built up field fortifications. One of the small teams led by Captain Amol Kalia from 5 PARA had been air-dropped in the vicinity on the previous day.

---

[*] All actions leading up to only the launch of an assault are called feint attack. It is only a show to deceive the enemy.

These troops used their mountaineering skills to reach the top and captured part of the locality before dawn. They immediately reorganized themselves to face counter-attacks.

The enemy came back in the morning and launched a fierce counter-attack. Captain Kalia's LMG detachment was fatally shot down. Captain Kalia picked up the LMG and fought, despite being injured himself. But the odds were against them. They were outnumbered. He along with his entire team went down fighting for their motherland. It was one of the bravest acts in this battle. He was awarded the Vir Chakra, posthumously, for this action in the face of the enemy. Sadly, his parents received a letter from him a day after his martyrdom stating that he was coming home on leave shortly and they could plan to get him married.

The rest of the troops continued to hold on to the top of Point 5203, but with the enemy occupying two ledges on the northwestern and southwestern slopes, it was imperative to rush more troops to Point 5203. Moving troops from elsewhere was difficult, as leaving any position unoccupied would have invited the enemy over to recapture it. Somehow, we managed to pull out a small body of men to strengthen the Top. The enemy, however, was still able to maintain its locations by bringing in supplies and ammunition by night.

The Ladakh Scouts are hardened troops and, being from the same region, their record of survival in isolated pockets was better than of any of the other troops present. They were, therefore, asked to establish blocks beyond Point 5203 in the area known as Boulders, to intercept the enemy's route of maintenance. One platoon under Captain Bishnoi did this job very effectively, blocking enemy movement from that direction. Meanwhile, the artillery continued to degrade the enemy's defences.

This situation lasted almost a week, but neither side was ready to withdraw. However, the intensity of fire from the enemy side had considerably reduced, suggesting that they were running low on ammunition, and also, perhaps, the will to fight. The time was ripe to launch the second phase of the operation but no troops were available close by for the next few days.

Meanwhile, one company of 5 PARA had captured a place known as Sunonpo Kadpego in a separate operation. Buoyed by their success, they were made available for this attack. Two additional companies of Ladakh Scouts were also released. By 20$^{th}$ June the second phase would be launched.

The attack was launched on the two slopes where the enemy was still holding out. In this operation, sixteen of our brave men were martyred and many were injured. However, the enemy fled from the location, leaving behind a large quantity of ammunition and personal clothing. Seventeen of their soldiers were killed in the attack, and our troops found their dead bodies strewn around, without much effort being made to bury them. The task of honouring their dead was also left to the Indian soldiers. The complete feature was secured by first light on 21$^{st}$ June.

After the clearance of Point 5203, the focus shifted back to the original objectives, to the west of Junk Lungpa. Minor modifications were made, in order to operate simultaneously on the western and eastern flanks, the plan being to link up at Point 5285 in the general area of Shangruti.

## Jintu in China Nala

On the western flank, the 17$^{th}$ Battalion of Garhwal Rifles (17 GARH RIF) was tasked with capturing Bump III and Saddle from the western direction, while 1 BIHAR was to link up with 17 GARH RIF in the north, after having captured the enemy localities on Jubar Complex.

The attack was planned for the night of 29$^{th}$ June. Accordingly, 17 GARH RIF reached the area around Tent in China Nala. Five days were available to them for build-up and reconnaissance.

The battalion was concentrated at Bakri Hut, a place used by

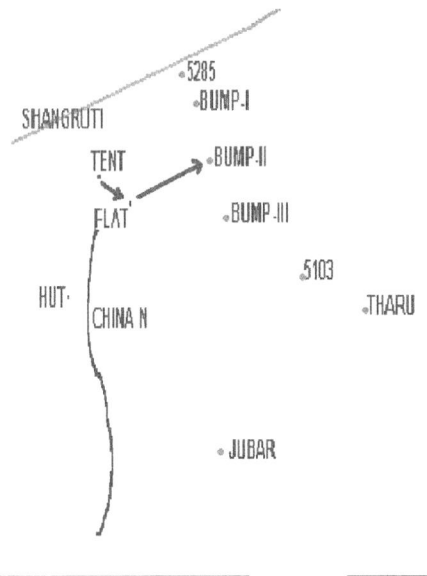

MAP 18: Battle for Bump III—17 Garhwal

Bakarwals to graze their animals during the summers. The plan was to capture the enemy positions of Bump III, Kalapathar and Mound, with a company each. These enemy positions were all located between Bump II and III where Para Special Forces had reached earlier (See 'Operations in Batalik-Yaldor'). By now, the enemy had had time to dig in and prepare well. The battalion planned to establish a firm base at a distance of 4–5 kilometres at a location known as Flat Area in China Nala, where they could carry out final preparations for the attack, and leave their heavy equipment behind. Time calculations had been carried out to ensure that movement from Bakri Hut to Flat Area, and then to the crest line where the enemy was positioned, was completed before the day broke.

The attacking columns commenced their movement in the last light of 29th June. On these Himalayan heights, frozen even during the peak of summer, an eerie silence prevailed. It was a full moon night and the sky was crystal clear. Temperatures had once again dipped well below the freezing point, making the advance extremely slow. A kilometre-long steep climb lay ahead before they could reach the crest line.

The company heading for Bump III encountered a huge rocky outcrop with boulders almost the size of a room. The companies heading for Kalapathar and Mound also got delayed due to the steep nature of the climb. The delay caused by the obstacles en route made them vulnerable to detection by the enemy in daylight.

Captain Jintu Gogoi was heading for Kalapathar. He had only two men behind him, with the rest struggling to cover the last 100 feet, a near vertical climb. Day had just broken when he reached the crest line. When he looked left, and then right, to locate the enemy bunker, he found a MMG was pointing straight at him!

As the moon shone over them, the enemy had quietly watched them come up, and waited patiently. When Gogoi reached the top, the enemy Platoon Commander shouted from his bunker, 'Aap Hindustan Army ke bahadur officer ho, par surrender kar do, aapko koi takleef nahin denge; varna main goli mar dunga!' (I know you are a brave officer; surrender, and we will not torture you; else, I will shoot you)

Jintu Gogoi was a man with nerves of steel, and was well known for being fearless. He knew what lay ahead. He ordered the troops following him to rush back to the firm base without waiting for him, while he would hold on to the enemy. Turning back to the bunker, he replied, 'Surrender main nahin, tum karoge; apni fikar karo!' (You will surrender, not me; watch out for yourself!)

Sadly, these were his last words before he fell to the enemy bullets.

Heavy casualties were avoided due to his self-sacrifice, but the attack was repulsed. The troops that had been following him made it back to the firm base, and remained in contact with the enemy for three nights thereafter. Jintu Gogoi was awarded the Vir Chakra, posthumously.

~

Major Jaitly was in charge of the company heading to Mound. They, too, were attacked as the daylight came. Fortunately, he only got injured in his leg. He ordered his men to fall back, but in the melee, the troops were scattered all over. His radio set malfunctioned due to damage during the firefight, and he could not contact the CO who had come up to the firm base at night from his Command Post in the New Tent area. There was no news from Major Jaitly for the next two nights—a cause of concern for the battalion. Despite being seriously wounded, only once all the men were accounted for, did Major Jaitly return to the base with his company.

Meanwhile, the company heading for Bump III had come under severe MMG fire. The tracer rounds could be seen all over, like fireflies darting across the mountains—an extraordinary spectacle, under normal circumstances. This company too, however, had to fall back without success.

The battalion remained in contact with the enemy for the next three nights. Thereafter, short of two companies, it moved back to Darchik.

Bump III was finally captured by 17 GARH RIF in the first week of July.

# Khalubar and Stangba Ridgelines

The Khalubar Ridgeline is in the Batalik Area. The Jubar Complex is to its left and Point 5203 to its right in the Chorbat La Area, close to the LOC. The highest feature is Point 5287 (approximately 16,000 feet), with Point 4812 in its vicinity towards the south (See Map 19). To reach the LOC, it was important to dislodge the enemy from there.

## Roar of Allah-hu-Akbar

The 22nd Battalion of the Grenadiers Regiment (22 GREN) arrived in the region in the third week of June 1999, straight from desert-oriented training! Now they were expected to scale and defend lofty Himalayan peaks. The battalion surely needed some time to adjust to the new environs, but there was hardly any time.

With minimum preparation and practically no mountain warfare training, Major Ajit Singh was given the task of gaining a foothold on the top, between the two heights—Point 5287 and Point 4812—by the morning of 1st July. A tall order, indeed! Earlier attempts had been made by other battalions from other directions, but none could succeed as the enemy was occupying the area in very heavy strength from those sides. The current approach to the objective area was quite steep, and equally dangerous, because the enemy could observe their movements.

The approach outlined for 22 GREN was the only available alternative yet to be tried out.

The time to start moving upwards towards the objective was set for after dark. However, even before the troops had assembled, heavy enemy fire came down upon them. The enemy's artillery was firing very accurately, truth be told. Heavy fire and the darkness made it difficult to regain command and control. A true soldier, however, never leaves the battlefield in the face of the enemy, and never shows his back to him. And so, Major Ajit took charge and within half an hour, had commenced movement upwards.

It was an extremely treacherous climb, as the gradient was steep and the boulders were slippery due to rain and snow. Also, the enemy sniper was picking off our soldiers one after the other, even at night. They could only advance from one boulder to another, till they reached a point from where they could not go upwards as there was a cliff in front and enemy fire from both sides.

The rumbling of stones was a loud and clear indication that the enemy was going to push boulders onto them. Their soldiers were so close that our men could hear them shouting out instructions to each other!

Injuries were bound to happen. Among others, Lance Havildar Shamshad was badly wounded and gasped for breath. A vigorous pounding of his chest eventually resuscitated him. However, carrying him to the higher reaches may have been detrimental to him apart from delaying the climb, but leaving him behind was not an option. The Indian Army does not abandon the wounded, or the dead. So, three experienced climbers from another battalion prepared a team to escort Lance Havildar Shamshad back to the base.

With daybreak a mere hour away, Major Ajit wondered if they were trapped for the day, only to be killed for sure. It was a 'now-or-never' situation, but he was not one to lose heart. The cliff *had* to be scaled. There was total silence and no one spoke, except Major Ajit.

'NARRA-E-TAQBIR' (Allah is the Greatest!), he proclaimed at the top of his voice. The brave boys of his company instantaneously and with equal gusto responded, 'ALLAH-HU-AKBAR!' With renewed strength, all hands got together to push one of them upwards, with the aid of a rope, till he managed a foothold. The remaining followed, in a similar manner, to the echoing cries of 'Narra-e-Taqbir' and 'Allah-hu-Akbar'.

The battle cry had a magical effect on the Pakistani soldiers too. They ceased firing. The rumbling and rolling down of stones stopped. Possibly they thought that these were their own men who had come to reinforce them!

Major Ajit and his boys—two dozen men, one Junior Commissioned Officer (JCO) and Second Lieutenant S.S. Shekhawat, who had just joined the battalion after training at the Academy—quickly reached the top. The first of July. A bright day. The glow of the sun helped in telling friend from foe.

However, the ordeal was far from over. In fact, yesterday's obstacles seemed easier. Their advance was fast paced though, and a lodgement of 50–60 metres was soon secured. The other side of the ridge was comparatively less steep, and one could peep into the rear side of the enemy's position. Major Ajit's keen eye spotted their helipad where additional manpower was landing. Something had to be done!

He saw a telephone line passing through the patch connecting the two shoulders. Major Ajit knew that the enemy was well entrenched and he had to disrupt their communications, so he cut their telephone line. The enemy responded by bringing down heavy fire from rocket launchers and MMGs. Our troops, though tired, continued to defend themselves with great alacrity.

By evening, two men were lost, and many injured. There was no sign of the troops meant to reinforce them or bring them their ammunition, food and sleeping bags. Rest and sleep became a distant dream. A bag full of pooris, however, did reach them through the trailing column of a few men that arrived. Three pooris each—enough to survive. A deep search of pockets brought forth chocolates that had been issued to them as part of their survival ration. This was the time for survival! The chocolates were energizers and morale boosters, putting smiles on their faces, and loving images of their young ones back home in their thoughts.

Respite was, however, short-lived. The enemy counter-attacked with double the number of men this time. As vigorous fighting was resumed, our troops started suffering losses of both men and the material which they had mustered at the top with great difficulty. Despite this, 22 GREN fought like hungry lions and succeeded in beating the enemy back.

The enemy seemed equally determined though. They returned with additional men after a short gap, but were once again unsuccessful in dislodging the brave Indian soldiers.

There was no rest for the next two days and nights. But the trying conditions did not deter either side. The din and the noise of the fire were so intense that one of the soldiers, Shafiq, who had a bullet pass though his helmet, didn't realize it for another two days! Hardly anyone remained untouched by injury. There were also serious casualties, as well as fatal ones. The soldiers could depend on nothing but their own grit, bravery and good luck.

Help came only on the third morning. A few Gorkha soldiers, under Colonel S.S. Rai who had taken over 1/11 GR as CO, managed to reach the top, followed by some more of their troops and a dozen Grenadiers. One MMG and an Automatic Grenade Launcher (AGL) had also been fetched up. This gave some solace to the beleaguered troops who had been continuously fighting for the last two days and three nights with almost no food or ammunition. Their trials and tribulations, however, were far from over. The sleeping bags had still not reached them and the injured soldiers struggled to keep themselves alive in sub-zero temperatures while the rest were busy fighting.

A quick attack was launched with this handful of fresh troops but they suffered casualties. The enemy launched yet another counter-attack in the afternoon. Fierce fighting ensued and the enemy and our troops were so intermingled among the boulders that there was utter confusion, compounded by fire from all sides. Our fighting strength was further depleted.

The enemy commander was hardly a few feet away. He called out aloud to our troops, asking them to surrender. He added that he would spare their lives and treat them well, were they to comply. He sounded so polite, genuine and convincing that anybody in that prolonged state of exhaustion and shock would have been tempted to surrender.

A shiver ran down Major Ajit's spine. It was imperative to restore faith and hope in his men, lest one among them inadvertently buckle in a moment of weakness. He did some quick thinking, and shouted back, 'Surrender karenge hum nahin, surrender karoge tum, kyoki hamare 150 jawan tumhare peechche se chadney mein kamyab ho gaye hain!' (You will be the ones surrendering, not us, because our 150 jawans have succeeded in climbing up behind you!)

This broke the lull in the battle and intense firing resumed. Just then, Shafiq, who still had a hole in his helmet, pointed out the enemy commander to Major Ajit. With his pulse racing, he looked up at the sky. The sun was fading and soon it would be night. Something had to be done quickly, or the fleeting opportunity would pass.

Major Ajit checked his rifle. There were only six bullets left. He immediately removed two bullets from the rifle magazine and kept them in his pocket. He fixed the bayonet on his rifle for hand-to-hand combat, if this ammunition too finished. Colonel Rai saw this and gave him a questioning look. Major Ajit indicated to him in sign language that it was meant to shoot himself in the head were he to fall into the hands of the enemy. The other bullet was a spare one, just in case the first one did not do the trick.

Everyone followed suit.

Major Ajit closed his eyes and bowed to his 'Kul-Devi', and pumped the four bullets into the gap between the boulders, putting an end to the surrender request. He had been one of the best shooters while training in the Indian Military Academy at Dehradun.

Bullets, however, continued to whiz by and a few seconds later, Naik Zakir Hussain, who had been performing the role of the Maulvi for a very long time, and had volunteered to man the light machine gun, was shot dead. He had successfully kept the enemy at bay continuously for sixty hours. Another brave soldier, Riyasat Ali, who was manning the MMG also got a bullet put through him, killing him on the spot. Unluckily, the AGL which had come up later had also got jammed and the entire ammunition was exhausted.

Seeing the end very close, Major Ajit was very rapidly scanning his mind to search for a solution. He remembered one of his instructors, a guru, who had trained him, and told him, 'When in trouble—remember God! Also, remember the artillery, and ask for fire support.'

A call for artillery SOS fire is given out as a last resort when there are no other options and the resultant casualties to own troops is grudgingly acceptable. This is done by giving out our own coordinates on the radio set. They were, as it is, too close to the enemy and would perhaps not make it. The thought flashed through Major Ajit's mind, would it not be better to lay down his life with own shelling, rather than getting captured by the enemy?

His request was agreed to and the artillery fire arrived within no time. The loud explosions created intense fire and smoke. Major Ajit's gamble had paid off. The enemy's counter-attack was repulsed, with heavy casualties to them. Our own troops suffered injuries as well.

With the fall of night, the firing ebbed, on both sides. Silence at last. The first time in almost four days.

~

Later in the night, the remaining Gorkha Regiment troops, who had lined up at the base by then, were to capture Bunker Ridge and a part of Khalubar Ridge, which was held by the enemy. The battle at Khalubar had already taken a heavy toll on our troops. One of the fallen was the younger brother of Lance Havildar Shamshad. How many more were there for whom the bell would toll?

# Lightning Bolt in the Sky at Bunker Ridge

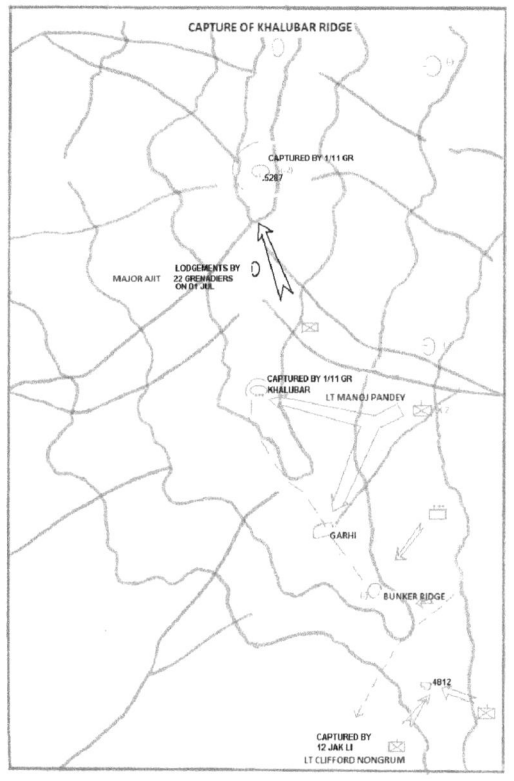

MAP 19: Capture of Khalubar Ridge

22 GREN had lodged a foothold on Khalubar Ridgeline between Point 5287 and Point 4812 under Major Ajit by 1st July. This offered an opportunity for two companies to pass through and facilitate the capture of Khalubar and Point 5287 the next night. Major Christopher Correya and Major Ajay Tomar under Colonel Lalit Rai, CO of 1st Battalion of the 11 Gorkha Regiment (1/11 GR), led this entire column.

## Aayo Gorkhali!

Gorkhas are one of the most ferocious troops in a battlefield. Their folklore suggests that once a khukri\* is taken out by the Gorkha soldier, it cannot not be sheathed until it is smeared red with the enemy's blood. The khukri-wielding Gorkha is feared the world over. A long history of participation in wars proves that they have stood out as one of the best martial races in the world.

The battalion had already gathered at the base of Point 4812. 12 JAK LI was poised nearby for a simultaneous attack on Point 4812. Reconnaissance patrols were sent to get information about the enemy's exact locations before the attack. One of the 1/11 GR patrols came under enemy fire and a soldier, Naik Gyanendra Rai, got injured and separated from his team.

Due to loss of blood he had become unconscious. He started hallucinating that he was surrounded by Pakistani soldiers. He felt someone was shaking him up vigorously; on regaining consciousness, he found himself surrounded by Pakistani soldiers in reality. They mocked him, asking him to wield his khukri. They were planning to take him to their unit and hang him upside down with it.

One of the Indian artillery officers happened to notice a group of Pakistani soldiers collected together. He decided to

---

\* A sharp-edged traditional knife, that is part of the uniform kit of a Gorkha soldier.

engage them with artillery fire without really realizing that they were milling around Naik Gyanendra Rai. This proved lucky for the half-conscious man; the Pakistanis dispersed quickly when the fire came. Naik Gyanendra quickly slipped into a nala nearby. He crawled down and hid behind boulders. Later, he got out without getting caught by Pakistanis. However, he could only manage to reach his battalion after two–three days of roaming around without food and medicines.

Meanwhile, Lt Manoj Pandey's party was part of Major Correya's column for the attack. He was tasked to clear Bunker Ridge while the balance of the Khalubar was being attacked by the rest of the troops. It was the night of $2^{nd}$ July, and his platoon led the advance towards Khalubar. As they reached the vicinity, the enemy opened heavy fire from all sides. They had reached the enemy's killing ground! Not to be disheartened, he managed to move his team to a position of advantage, and identified the area from where the maximum fire was coming—six bunkers were spitting fire upon them.

He noticed that someone was trying to attract his attention from two of those bunkers, shouting as if they were their own troops. Shouting at each other, they communicated that they were from the Indian Army and belonged to some Guards Unit. For a moment, Lt Pandey was in two minds: should he go closer and shake hands, or should he fire at them? However, he felt that there was something amiss… A flash of memory alerted him that no such Guards Unit was operating anywhere near this area! He let off bullets from his rifle and the enemy quickly ducked back into their bunkers.

Lt Pandey took a quick decision and split his platoon into three teams. He asked one of them to support their advance, while the team under Havildar Bhim Bahadur was to charge two of the bunkers. His own team was to rush towards the four remaining bunkers to his left; he chose to take the toughest part for himself.

'Aayo Gorkhali!' the battle cry of the Gorkha Regiment, echoed louder than the sounds of explosions around. Fierce fighting continued, and at places, hand-to-hand battles occured; the khukri blade shone every now and then like a lightning bolt on the skyline. Lt Pandey was fearless. He assaulted the bunkers, and one after the other, he killed four enemy soldiers.

After clearing the first two bunkers, he did not stop to breathe, and headed for the next. At the third one, he was wounded in his shoulder and leg, but without bothering about his injury, he charged menacingly towards the fourth bunker. 'Aayo Gorkhali!' roared in the air. He pulled out a hand grenade and lobbed it through the loophole in the bunker from where a MMG was rapidly firing. Unfortunately, one of its bursts hit his forehead.

The hand grenade he had lobbed into the loophole found its target, and all the occupants of the fourth bunker were silenced, forever. All six bunkers were now empty and almost a dozen enemy soldiers' bodies were strewn around the ridge.

Lt Manoj Pandey had sacrificed his life to gain a foothold on Bunker Ridge. He had joined the battalion recently, after going through training at the NDA in Khadakwasla, Pune and then at the Indian Military Academy, Dehradun. Early in life, Manoj had decided that he would like to be a military officer. He had always cherished the idea of doing great things for his country one day. He joined Sainik School, Lucknow at an early age, before going to the NDA. His father, Gopi Chand, and especially his mother, Mohini Pandey, played a big role in inculcating this spirit in him.

He had shown his mettle as a greenhorn officer when, immediately after joining his battalion in Kashmir prior to the onset of the Kargil war, he had accompanied his senior, Second Lt P.N. Dutt, who was awarded the Ashok Chakra, the country's highest award for bravery in operations other than war.

Lt Pandey had volunteered to cancel his Young Officers' course when his battalion went to the Siachen glacier. There, he had chosen the highest post for himself in the northern glacier, at a height of 19,700 feet. Only daredevils go there since, to reach it, one needs to cross a very narrow tunnel cut through the ice. Once inside, there's no turning back!

His seniors and colleagues would say that he needed anchors to restrain him lest he overstretch himself and went overboard. He demonstrated this spirit amply, and made not only his mother proud, but the entire motherland. A soldier's ultimate dream.

Lt Manoj Pandey was awarded the highest honour in the battlefield, the Param Vir Chakra. He has left behind a legacy, difficult to emulate, let alone surpass. He shall remain the shining star he was, forever.

~

Bunker Ridge now served as a vital launchpad for further operations. Reinforcements were sent under the battalion's second-in-command, Lt Col A. Asthana. The troops on Bunker Ridge reorganized themselves and were regrouped.

It was the turn of Khalubar Main. A fierce battle followed, for the next two days, and Khalubar fell by the third day, well before the morning. Similarly, Garhi also fell by the afternoon on the same day.

The next night, the attack on Point 5287 was pressed home, to maintain the momentum and not allow the enemy any respite, to either recoup or recover. Finally, with the capture of Point 5287, the entire Khalubar Ridgeline was clear of the enemy.

# Rising of the Eastern Star

While the operations to establish lodgements on Point 5287 and Point 4812 on Khalubar Ridgeline were progressing, yet another attack was being launched on Point 4812 by 12 JAK LI. The battalion, under Colonel V.S. Bhalothia, employed two companies to assault the enemy from the south and southeast under Major Dhiman and Pathak, and Lt Clifford Nongrum. The attack was launched on the night of 30th June. The enemy was well entrenched and offered very stiff resistance.

## Capture of Point 4812

Lt Keishing Clifford Nongrum, a young officer from Meghalaya, had been given responsibility for attacking a near-vertical cliff feature of Point 4812, to pave a way up. A near impossible task for anyone, but not for Clifford. He was determined to take up the challenge. He led the thirty soldiers of his platoon upwards. They steadily climbed the steep slope and reached the top.

The enemy bunkers at the top presented a rare view; they had carved out boulders and stones to make bunkers which connected with each other. It takes months to do such a job with stone-cutting machines. Our artillery had been firing at these bunkers, but no matter how intense the fire was, it did not affect them. Also, since they were interconnected, it was difficult to pull the enemy out from these bunkers and tackle them.

Suddenly, all hell broke loose. The enemy opened up with automatic machine gun fire and brought heavy mortar bombs to bear on Lt Nongrum and his platoon. When such a situation arises, the only way to succeed is to first go down to the ground, observe the enemy, and then fire. And so, Lt Clifford Nongrum remained pinned down to the ground for the next two hours before he could gather his complete platoon and indicate they should support his assault while he stood up to ferociously charge towards the nearest bunker firing at them.

Firing his rifle with one hand, and with a ready hand grenade in the other (he had pulled out the safety pin), he managed to reach the bunker and lobbed the hand grenade into it. With a loud explosion, the enemy soldiers inside the bunker went silent.

Lt Nongrum had not realized that he, too, was bleeding profusely. Although severely injured, he continued to fight hand-to-hand with the remaining enemy soldiers in the next bunker. His men knew that he was a boxer and could knock anyone out. He rushed towards the machine gun and attempted to snatch it from the hands of the enemy. In this fist fight, he shot the enemy dead. What he had not realized was that the barrel of the gun in the hands of a Pakistani soldier was pointing towards him, with his finger on the trigger. Lt Clifford Nongrum was again shot, and this time he collapsed immediately. Despite being wounded once, he had not halted, and chose to fight valiantly on the battlefield till his last breath.

Lt Keishing Clifford Nongrum was awarded the Maha Vir Chakra for this valiant act in the face of the enemy. He was the only officer from Meghalaya to have been awarded such an honour. A couple of years later, his father, Peter Keishing, paid homage to his son at the very spot where he had single-handedly killed several enemy soldiers. He came back deeply touched, moved and proud of his son who had made the supreme sacrifice for his motherland.

~

Major Pathak, who was attacking from a different approach nearby, was also stuck due to heavy enemy fire from the same point, as well as from Garhi nearby. He was, however, successful in capturing a Pakistani soldier, Naik Inayat Ali, who was taken as a Prisoner of War (PoW). Later, after the war, he was handed over to Pakistan following the Geneva Convention's provisions about PoWs, but not before being given five packets of cigarettes as a return gift for sharing a cigarette with an Indian counterpart when in custody. Despite sustaining himself for nearly ninety-six hours, Major Pathak could not advance due to the bad terrain and heavy enemy fire. All the troops pulled back, on orders, to replenish themselves.

The attack was reinforced the next day, with two fresh columns, from the south and southeast. Fierce fighting followed with the renewed attack. Eventually, Point 4812 fell into our hands by 6$^{th}$ July. The martyrdom of Lt Clifford Nongrum and others was not in vain. A new eastern star had risen in the sky, to shine forever.

# Stangba—Point 5000—Padma Go—Dog Hill

In the close vicinity of the Khalubar Ridgeline, and towards the LOC, stands Stangba area with Point 5000, Padma Go and Dog Hill. All these areas needed to be cleared of the enemy. Two companies of Indus Wing Ladakh Scouts were tasked to capture Padma Go and Point 5000.

The time to launch the attack was once again at night, the night of 30th June; Major Ajit was also assaulting at the same time (See 'Khalubar and Stangba Ridgelines'). Movement towards Point 5000 was rapid and with some effort it was captured and occupied. The route to Padma Go offered steep cliffs and escarpments close to the objective, and there was no way to bypass it. Urgent steps needed to be taken lest the enemy further strengthen this location.

A commander in war has to plan for all the possible contingencies that may arise; the plan was therefore modified. Point 5000 was kept occupied by creating an ad-hoc company and, instead of Padma Go, Dog Hill became the next objective to be assaulted. The firefighting took place there, but the Ladakh Scouts were sharper in using the terrain to their advantage, as they were from the region. They forced the enemy to start withdrawing. Dog Hill was captured on the fifth night.

~

Padma Go, the last objective in the vicinity, stood tall with another feature called Knoll. Two companies, under Major John Lewis and Captain Bishnoi, were assigned one objective each. It took considerable time to reach these areas while under enemy fire. Once on the objective, fierce battles developed at both the places. Mention must be made of Tashi Nugyal and his team, who were part of this assaulting column. They displayed utmost bravery in this part of the battle. By midday on 9th July, both Knoll and Padma Go were finally cleared of the enemy.

A wounded Pakistan Army soldier was captured in the area. He was visibly relieved to be caught as a Prisoner of War by the Indian troops and thanked them for their generosity and food, as he was hungry. He was given first aid and transferred to the military hospital in the rear. Later, he was handed over to Pakistan.

As in the Dras and Mashkoh area, the enemy had been cleared from Chorbat La in the east by simultaneous attacks launched on Stangba area, Khalubar Ridgeline and Point 4812. The enemy was spotted withdrawing without any attack developing from the Indian side by our soldiers. The Ladakh Scouts had earned their badges of honour, and continued to protect not only their homeland but also their motherland.

The contribution of the people of Ladakh to the Kargil war effort is immense; they took pride in voluntarily supporting the battle-weary troops. The Ladakh Buddhist Association deserves a special mention, as they ensured that all, irrespective of status, were deployed to carry loads of rations turn-by-turn for their soldiers, right up to the peaks, under freezing conditions and enemy fire. They would insist on going ahead and delivering the loads, considering it their sacred duty towards the saviours of their land—an indelible mark of patriotism.

It was a matter of time before the complete area in Batalik-Yaldor and Chorbat La was cleared of the enemy, right up to the LOC.

# The Glorious Siachen Glacier
## Nothing but Excellence

Point 5770 is a part of the Southern Siachen Glacier which was held by Pakistan. This post was important for Pakistan, as it provided a view of Mian Lungpa through which Pakistan developed a major attack during the Kargil operations. Any movement in this part of Siachen Glacier was unsafe as long as the Pakistanis sat there.

Earlier attempts to capture Point 5770 had not succeeded, due to the cliff that rose 1,800 feet above the rest. There was no safe access to this cliff except a gradual slope that was the Pakistani side. Reaching the top of this feature was almost an 80-degree treacherous climb involving negotiations of overhangs and icy blue cornices. Although the left and right shoulders of this feature were held by our troops, movement by day or even by night was extremely difficult, as any move would invite heavy fire.

The 27$^{th}$ Battalion of the Rajput Regiment (27 RAJPUT) commanded by Colonel Konsam Himalaya Singh had just arrived in Siachen from Delhi. True to his name, he had chosen to bring the battalion to the Himalayan peaks of glory. He tasked Major Navdeep Cheema with capturing this post around mid-June.

A plan was made to climb this height by fixing ropes, for which a special team under Captain Shyamal Sinha of the High-Altitude Warfare School was constituted. The attacking troops could catch hold of these ropes and climb the cliff. But the danger of the enemy noticing the fixing of the ropes forced them to adopt a more difficult alternative, in which the ropes were to be fixed under an ice overhang. It was to be negotiated by each soldier, physically hanging on to the ropes, and moving ahead by using only his hands. A very tough thing to do, even in normal conditions!

At 18,000 feet, with temperatures plunging down to minus 40 degrees Celsius, even a trained mountaineer requires unfathomable courage to negotiate an overhang in mid-air. And that's with no enemy around to shoot him! But these men were made of steel to have even thought of doing so.

Another problem that unfolded was that a total of thirty such ropes were required, and there were not enough available in the entire Siachen Glacier. Quick staff work at the HQ came to their rescue. An aircraft and helicopters, in chain, specially flew in the desired ropes all the way across the Himalayas, well before the end of the following day.

On 25th June, the ropes were finally in place. The element of surprise was lost but at first light, as the troops started to march ahead, a snow blizzard dropped visibility to below one metre. The attack plan had to be postponed.

Finally, on 27th June, six bravehearts, including two specialists to fix the ropes, led by Major Cheema and Captain Sinha, respectively, proceeded to launch the attack on Point 5770. Captain Sinha and his team successfully fixed the ropes. By midday, Major Cheema and four soldiers started their journey up these ropes to the top of Point 5770. Their progress was painfully slow due to the extreme cold, steep climb and the presence of icy cornices and overhangs. A small mistake could have landed not one, but the entire team, hanging onto the rope, several hundred feet below, in the icy crevasses.

Fortune favoured these braves, and the steady climb ultimately ended with Major Cheema reaching the top—only to find himself in front of an enemy sentry who was writing a letter, sitting next to his Universal Machine Gun (UMG).

Although out of breath, Cheema could see that the enemy sentry had seen him come up and was about to grab his UMG to fire at him! There was no time to regain breath; with frozen hands, Cheema pressed the trigger of his weapon, and killed the sentry before he could react. The sound of the firing alerted the other members of the enemy party. Cheema now rushed ahead and turned the enemy's UMG against them. It was only a few minutes before ten to fifteen of the enemy were lying dead around him and his men, who had come up right behind him. Some of the enemy soldiers managed to run away from there, to carry the tale of their disaster to others down below in Pakistan.

A large number of Pakistani arms and huge amounts of ammunition and rations were recovered. The letters found on their bodies revealed the identity of the dead. Our own team did not suffer a single casualty, by the fall of night on 27$^{th}$ June.

The dead Pakistani soldiers were buried there itself. At a special request made by a Pakistani mother later, one of the dead bodies was exhumed. It was the body of an officer whose father had fought the 1971 Indo-Pak war. The body was handed over to Pakistan, as a mark of respect to the soldier. This was in sharp contrast to what Pakistan had done to the dead body of Lt Kalia at Bajrang Post in Kaksar (See p. 36).

Major Cheema was awarded the Sena Medal for his exceptional bravery. A Vir Chakra was awarded to Captain Shyamal Sinha who had fixed the ropes under such enormously testing conditions.

> Soldier, rest! thy warfare o'er,
> Sleep the sleep that knows not breaking;
> Dream of battlefields no more,
> Days of danger, nights of waking.
> — Sir Walter Scott

# Epilogue

By the first week of July 1999, it was clear to the Pakistani military commanders and political leadership that their latest military misadventure had fizzled out. Pakistani troops on the ground were paying dearly for their follies as the Indian Army was making substantial gains every day. If immediate steps were not taken by Pakistan, their troops inside Indian Territory faced complete annihilation and rout at the hands of the Indian Army.

The ground position by the first week of July was that Pakistan's plans to launch a major offensive in Turtok-Chalunka had been blunted. The enemy was contained and it was beyond their capability to make any progress across the Line of Control. In Chorbat La, all positions on the LOC east of Point 5440 were already occupied by the Ladakh Scouts, and were subsequently relieved by a regular battalion.

By the first week of July, in Yaldor sector on the Western flank, our troops had encircled the enemy and were in contact at Bump II, a point very close to the LOC. The operations to capture Jubar Complex and Tharu and Kukar Thang were already over. On the Khalubar Ridge, Point 5000 had fallen on 1$^{st}$ July, while Khalubar itself fell on 4$^{th}$ July. With the capture of Point 5287 and Garhi by 5$^{th}$ July, the enemy defences on Khalubar and Stangba Ridge had fallen to the might of Indian Army. Jubar Main was captured on 7$^{th}$ July and Jubar Top fell on 8$^{th}$ July. In further progress in the Western flank, Bump III fell on 7th July. Indian troops had reached behind the enemy and they were completely encircled.

The enemy had also been more or less completely thrown out in Dras, and Indian troops had reached the LOC by capturing Three Pimples and Point 4700 by 29th June. Tiger Hill, perhaps the greatest psychological victory, fell on 4th July 1999.

At the same time, in Mashkoh Valley, Point 4875, the most dominating and important objective, was captured by 7th July. The enemy in this sector too was completely encircled. On the western flank of Mashkoh Valley, own troops were within a kilometre of the LoC, while the Pakistani administrative base located at Point 4388, which was the epicentre of supplies in the Dras-Mashkoh Sector, was in the process of being captured.

The enemy was still approximately 2.5 kilometres inside our territory, only in Kaksar. That was because it was last in the priority of conducting operations; it was to be tackled after the situation in other sectors was restored.

Thus, by the first week of July, senior officers had begun to visit to witness glimpses of the Pakistani rout. The Chief of Army Staff visited Yaldor, Batalik and Ganasok, 500 metres short of the LOC on 7th July.

~

Sensing their imminent disastrous defeat at the hands of 15 Corps of the Indian Army, Nawaz Sharif, the Prime Minister of Pakistan was forced to rush first to China and then to the USA. He was snubbed at both the places. Seeing no light at the end of the tunnel, and having been isolated on the international platform, while his army faced a complete rout, the Pakistani prime minister was forced to accept yet another blow to national pride after the Indo-Pak War of 1971. It was thus very evident that the Pakistan Army was on the run owing to its continuous defeat on the ground. To avoid being exposed completely on the international forum, they disguised their defeat by giving it the form of a withdrawal. The only place where they needed to actually withdraw was in Kaksar, where the operations of Indian Army had not yet begun with full might. Fearing death, destruction and annihilation of Pakistani troops, Pakistan proposed to withdraw from this area first.

Consequently, on 9th July 1999, in a telephonic conversation between the two Director Generals of Military Operations (DGMOs) on the hotline, the Pakistani DGMO proposed pulling out in a phased manner. It was decided to first vacate the Kaksar intrusion, starting from first light on 10th July to first light on 12th July. Pulling out from other sectors was to start once the pull-out from Kaksar was verified. It was also agreed upon that no air attack or artillery/mortar fire would be carried out in the areas of withdrawal, and no assaults would be launched from 9th July onwards in other sectors. No restriction was, however, imposed upon the firing of other weapons.

On 11 July 1999, Major General Tauqir Zia, the Pakistani DGMO met Lt Gen N.C. Vij, PVSM, AVSM and the Indian DGMO at the Wagah border. He offered that Pakistani troops would pull out from Mashkoh from 12th to 15th July. The pull-out from Dras would begin from 14th July, and was to be completed by 15th July. In the Batalik-Yaldor Sector, up to Turtok, the pull-out would begin on 15th July and was to be completed by 16th July. As a matter of fact, in all these sectors, there were hardly any areas where the Pakistani Army had a toehold; they only wanted to pull out the remnants and the equipment.

It was also agreed that no new posts were to be held within 1000 metres of the LOC, on either side.

Due to their past record, it was anticipated that Pakistan would not withdraw. The apprehension was that they would use this time to lay mines, reinforce their positions and strengthen their locations. These apprehensions proved to be correct when Pakistan breached the understanding by delaying the withdrawal and used this time to lay mines and extricate heavy stores and weapons. Pakistan did not withdraw from the Turtok area, and continued to hold on to certain positions across the LOC in Batalik, Dras and Mashkoh sub-sectors. They also inducted fresh regular troops.

These intrusions had to be evicted by launching physical assaults to restore the sanctity of Line of Control. Operation Vijay officially terminated on July 26$^{th}$, 1999.

# An Ode to the Indian Soldier

By Major A.R. Ramakrishnan, Company Commander
in Kargil

The silence of the Winter Snow
Settles over our land, we know,
High over in valleys, the peaks
Blood is the only language that speaks.

Emotion, esprit-de-corp's oozing
Out of each ones' *heart*.
Another soldier upward *he* starts.

They were marching up
In hoards, in swarms
To wipe out the aggressor's qualms

They formed, they led,
They swept in waves to
Forever seal
To catch the uncanny Fox
In his misadventures,
    zeal

So, what,
When, Why and where
They were reduced to a *naught*.

# An Ode to the Indian Soldier

Billions of us
Who know not
*their names*

For the Indian soldiers
Marches Ever onward
Never for *wealth,*
Never for *momentary fame*
For All the Millions
He Just Gave a Call
For I Gave My Tomorrow
For You All.

# Acknowledgements

Ever since my commissioning into the Indian Army, Kargil has beckoned me time and again and has become a major part of my life. Before Kargil, during the war and beyond, I have had the singular opportunity to interact and work with most of the Kargil commanders at all levels and with many of the men who valiantly fought there. Lest the valour of soldiers in Kargil is lost to our posterity I have endeavoured to write this book based upon my personal interactions. This current account of the Kargil war is an acknowledgement of my deepest respect towards these men, who fought or contributed in Kargil, thus saving the frontiers of our sacred land through their sweat and blood.

Several seniors, colleagues, friends and relatives had urged me to undertake this historic journey down memory lane. The list is very long and the few pages here will not suffice to list them all. I sincerely thank each one of them to have had the faith in me and belief in my capabilities to deliver it. I would, however, be failing on my part if I do not mention General V.P. Malik, PVSM, AVSM, (Retd), the former Chief of the Army Staff, who has consistently supported me on this venture. Mention of Lt Gen Krishan Pal, GOC 15 Corps, Lt Gen Mohinder Puri, PVSM, UYSM (Retd), Lt Gen Amar Aul, PVSM, AVSM, UYSM (Retd), Maj Gen VS Budhwar (Retd), Brig Devinder Singh (Retd), Brig R.K. Kakar and a long list of Commanding Officers, Company Commanders, Post Commanders, Team

# Acknowledgements

Leaders and soldiers who fought there is important. They spared their valuable time in personal discussions with me.

My team at the Corps Battle School deserves special credit and I am indebted to the contributions made by Lt Col Manoj Chaturvedi, Major (Late) Ram Singh Kadiyan and Major Subbiah Kailasam who accompanied me in the battle zone during the various stages of war and stood by me to help me complete the research afterwards.

I had the opportunity to interact with the American and Pakistani academic community at the Centre for Contemporary Conflict Studies, Monterey, California, USA when I was invited to present my research papers during the Research Fellowship at the USI of India for their Project on compiling 'Asymmetric Warfare in South Asia: Kargil 1999 and Beyond'. The exposure came in handy to understand the different narratives and perspectives around the Kargil war.

I thank Lt Gen P.K. Singh, PVSM, AVSM (Retd) the Director USI of India, Major General Y.K. Gera (Retd), Maj Gen P.K. Goswami, VSM (Retd) and Sqn Ldr Rana T.S. Chinna, (Retd), MBE without whose support I would not have been able to finally deliver the book.

Special references are deserved by Ms Minnoo Singh and I am immensely indebted to her for extreme dedication, commitment and hard work in polishing my written account, correcting and advising me on every step in writing this book.

Through this book, I pay my tributes to my late parents, who allowed and supported me to be a part and parcel of the armed forces fraternity and brotherhood. My mother took pride in my Kargil tenures and always blessed me. My very special gratitude is reserved for my wife, Poonam, who has been part of this journey and supported me all along. She has never flinched or complained of my long absences, whether on the war front or on routine and current work engagements, and has brought up both my daughters Pallavi and Shailvi with the same set of high values as her. I thank both my sons-in-law, Anshuman and Govind, who have been great supporters, admirers and most importantly critics of my work.

Last but not the least, I pay my deep regards to all the soldiers for upholding the glorious traditions and values we cherish in the Indian Armed Forces.

**Col S.C. Tyagi (Retd)**
New Delhi,
February 2019

www.ingramcontent.com/pod-product-compliance
Lightning Source LLC
Chambersburg PA
CBHW052051220426
43663CB00012B/2520